Just like mother used to make

Tom Norrington-Davies

For Ma, Pa, Danny and Jojo, with all my love

Just like mother used to make

Tom Norrington-Davies

photographs by Jason Lowe

First published in 2003 by Cassell Illustrated,
a division of Octopus Publishing Group Ltd

This edition published in 2005 exclusively for Marks and Spencer p.l.c

www.marksandspencer.com

A CIP catalogue record for this book is available from the British Library.

ISBN 1 84403 4275
EAN 9781844034277

Edited by Barbara Dixon
Photographs by Jason Lowe
Design by Simon Wilder
Jacket design by Jo Knowles

Printed in China

Acknowledgements

This book is based so much on the anecdotes of others that I can barely claim to have written it. First and foremost, I must express my profound gratitude to all my family, who have been amazing archivists. I should single out Mum, Dad, Annan, Aunty Mary, Mrs Norry, Nanny and Grandad.

I am forever indebted to Mike Belben for his tireless support and encouragement; Carla Tomasi for continued inspiration and guidance; Ruth Quinlan for a shove in the right direction; Danny Riordan for being up the road and 'Jelly' for (almost) never being bored.

For making it all happen I would like to thank: Lizzy Kremer and Grianne Fox at Ed Victor; Camilla Stoddart and Victoria Alers-Hankey at Cassell; Jason Lowe; John Bentham; Jacky Malouf; Polly Powell (for her kitchen) and Nigel Kidd (for mine).

And many thanks to the following for all their help and information: Lisa Belben; Ben's Fish; Julian Birch; Haley Brent-Isherwood; Jenny Butterworth; Adrian Capp; Simon Casson; Lori, John and Dawn Clements; Jane Davidson; Dorothy and Maurice De St Jorre; Will Eaves; Julian Eardley; David Eyre; Euan Ferguson; Fenella Fitch; Kathryn Flett; John Geddes; Mike Gee; Charlie Hicks; Trish Hilferty; Maxwell Hutchinson; Mary, Mark and Paul Johnstone; Gary Keiliff; Mark Jones; Annie Kelley; Amy Lamé; Nicki and Christopher Leggard; Harry Lester; Wendy Leston; Pat Llewellyn; Charles and James Mash; Corinne McCulloch; McKanna Meats; Jenny Mayers; Ros and Rosemary Moore; Neal's Yard Dairy; Litty Paxton; Jan and Mat Phillips; Gerald D. Preston; Leisa Rea; Lizzie Roper; Andy Ross; Wendy Sayell; David S. Taylor; Lee Tredera; Greg Wallace; Ashley Wallington; Jane Watson; Jenny Wayne; John and Jackie Williams; Lucia Withers; Mark Wood.

Last but not least the staff at the Eagle and the Fox (gold dust, every one).

Contents

Introduction. This is a book inspired by the food my mother and perhaps your mother used to make. It is a book about treating yourself to good old-fashioned comfort food. At first glance, some of the recipes will seem gloriously fuddy duddy. I personally want them to stay that way. I am not about to tell you that Shepherd's Pie is the latest in Retro Chic, nor will I urge you to rush out and buy masses of tupperware. Although some recipes might raise a smile, the food in this book is no joke.

The notion that food in Britain was a joke until about twelve years ago is one so often repeated that it has become a cliché. In our modern whirl of stir-fries and sushi, gulping down our cappuccinos and raw energy juices, we seem to have abandoned the foodie part of our national heritage. Boring old meat 'n' two veg, like school dinners (eugh!) have been dumped on a sort of mental scrap heap, along with wet, windy summers by the seaside. We've moved on.

By the end of the 1980s more of us were travelling abroad than ever before. As we munched our first rocket salads and pulled the funny little twigs out of Thai curries it was collectively decided that, unlike our dodgy weather, our cuisine could be re-invented. Perhaps we could sneak a little sunshine into our kitchens, if not our back yards. Then came the news that, while beer and butter were going to send you to an early grave, red wine and olive oil could help you live forever. That settled it. British Chefs (with a few exceptions) turned Tuscany into the centre of the Universe, then scoured ever more exotic corners of the globe, on a wild goose chase for any culinary tradition other than their own.

Truth be told, the British have always been magpies when it comes to food, grabbing all that tasted novel and exciting. Spices from the Far East and Africa were reaching Britain as long ago as the Middle Ages, and very little of what came out of our kitchens was ever free of influences from afar. The British palate suffered during and after the two world wars of the last century. Periods of enforced austerity put much of what was great about this eclectic cuisine on the back burner. Of course many of the culinary habits forced on us as a nation after the wars left a positive lasting impression on the way we were fed as children, and this is why we tend to relegate food from that time of our lives to the back of the pantry, as it were.

When the idea for a book about comfort eating was put to me I was instantly uneasy about this much abused term. By the end of the twentieth century we had developed a nasty habit of renaming any form of indulgence in pretend, psychiatrist terms. Thus, unnecessary shopping had become 'retail therapy', and snacking on anything stodgier than a tortilla wrap was 'comfort eating'. Worse still, this 'comfort eating' has become widely associated with the consumption of junk food. Because so many people rely on convenience and speed in the kitchen these days, our best intentions to eat healthily and wholesomely often fall by the wayside. We then joke that we are 'comfort eating' to somehow excuse this.

So what is real comfort eating? The answer is surely different for everyone, but because it often revolves around meals that are sweet or filling (or both), comfort eating and childhood are bound up with one another. Taste and smell are huge memory triggers, so it is not surprising that the poor, stressed out grown up of today might enjoy being transported back to the age of innocence by a dish of steaming mashed potatoes. What he or she may not realise is that if that mash comes from a packet of dried granules, something is missing from the experience.

Comfort eating is one thing. Comfort cooking is another. Leaving the kitchen with something good on your plate and a sense of achievement is comfort cookery. The worst thing about the current prevalence of convenience food is the idea that all cooking is a waste of your precious time. I am not about to start a rant about convenience food. I indulge in it more often than I'd like to but in fact I grew up in a home where it was pretty much outlawed, and I am grateful for that. It showed me that the enjoyment of eating is not exclusive to the home made tag, but that it is enhanced by the rituals of preparation. I still see that relationship when any number of the family is home at the same time. My mother, knowing that her clan is gathering, is almost certain to prepare food that will reaffirm her role as provider when we were small. My favourite childhood dish, or my brother's, may appear at the table. And these meals are some of the best in the world.

The preparation of food in my parents' house was often a communal affair. They both believed it was essential that their children would leave home knowing how to fend for themselves in the kitchen. As soon as we were old enough there was a loose rotation of the family's resident chefs. This hands-on knowledge of my mother's repertoire would stave off any unbearable bouts of homesickness once we flew the nest.

So, this book could be described as a collection of 'family favourites', food from the days when cookery was more about feeding and nurturing than impressing one another. As old-fashioned as some recipes may seem, this is no 'aga saga'. I have rescued many of the meals from what I call slavish authenticity. Cooking is about constant change and evolution. There seemed little point, in this day and age, in consulting Hannah Glasse or Mrs Beeton when I had a wealth of friends all of whom have their own stories to tell.

Then there are the constraints on peoples' time and kitchen space that a modern day food writer would be a fool to ignore. I have, for instance, had to try out most of these recipes in my shoebox of an urban kitchen. What's more, I cannot just follow a recipe, which is a failing of many chefs. I constantly cheat, skip, substitute and I am obsessed with saving time.

So I have modified and modernized; I have avoided gadgetry but most of all I have avoided anything that resembles restaurant food. This book is about home cooking. It should be easy enough for grown ups, children, and people like me (sort of grown-up children) to follow. After all, most of it is about the first kind of food that we learned to cook and eat, just like mother used to make.

Tom Norrington-Davies

Daytime

A dozen eggs. Eggs don't just make great comfort food. They are quick and easy to prepare and, packing a considerable nutritional punch, they can be good for you too. Yet few foods have received as much bad press as eggs in recent years. It is a shame that we have turned something so naturally good and simple to eat into such a nightmare.

Whether your chief worry is salmonella (food poisoning), cholesterol levels or fat content there is always something awful or confusing to contemplate when it comes to eggs. They do contain a certain amount of fat and cholesterol (the issue of whether this is good or bad seems to ignite most debates among nutritionists). What is beyond doubt, however, is that they contain a wealth of protein, minerals and vitamins that can be beneficial to you

I do not believe it is the place of a recipe book to dish out advice that pretends to be nutritionally foolproof in any way. Besides, opinions on eggs and their merits (or lack of them) change all the time. There are dozens of egg recipes in this book. It follows that if you are eating those meals every single day then you are probably eating too many eggs. In fact, you are eating too much rich, stodgy food, full stop.

There are also recipes for uncooked and only-just cooked eggs in this book. I have been making things like real mayonnaise for years with no problems. I can't responsibly tell you to do as I do here, but I believe I have had no problems because I buy, store and use eggs with a certain amount of caution. This has as much to do with taste and ethics as it does with health. I only ever use free-range, organic eggs, from small-scale producers. Eggs that do not have the words 'free' or 'range' on the packet are out of bounds for me. Apart from being a cruel and inhumane way of keeping hens, battery farming produces eggs that taste inferior. If you are not bothered about the treatment of hens this is as good a reason for buying free-range or organic eggs as any.

I buy from stores or farms that can give me a full and honest account of how the hens that laid the eggs are being kept and what they are fed on. They do cost more, but I only buy them when I am going to eat them. Eating eggs in moderation should negate the need to have vast amounts of them lying around waiting to be used, and won't break the bank. Sadly, it is not possible to wander into a large supermarket and pick up any old box of eggs without risking being misled by the packaging. At the risk of sounding Orwellian, some eggs are more free-range than others. Take the time to find out as much as you can about the producer.

Storing eggs. Eggs do not keep any better in a fridge than at a moderate temperature. The part of the kitchen that is coolest is best. If you have a pantry or larder then this is the best environment for them. Storing eggs for anything longer than two weeks is not a good idea as they lose flavour and texture.

Soft-boiled eggs and soldiers.

How do you boil an egg to perfection? Everyone has their own way, and here, without fanfare or much in the way of explanation, is mine. It works for me every time so I'm passing it on.

Heat a pan of salted water and when it has come to a rolling boil gently lower in as many eggs as you need. Watch them like a hawk. When the water has come back to the boil, time the eggs for 4 minutes if large and 3 minutes if medium. Lift them straight out of the water and eat immediately. Don't wait around for toast, have it ready, cut into strips narrow enough to dip into the eggs.

For hard-boiled eggs, put them in cold water, bring to the boil and simmer for 7 minutes if the eggs are large, and 6 minutes if they are smaller.

Hard-boiled eggs and soldiers is a waste of time. How, and where, will you dip the toast?!

Scrambled eggs.

Real scrambled eggs are not beaten in advance, but broken into the pan. Each to his or her own about how far to take them. I favour mine on the sloppy side.

For 4 people, melt 1 tablespoon of butter in a heavy-bottomed saucepan. When it has melted pour in 100ml/3½fl oz of milk and add a pinch of salt and pepper. Heat until the milk is scalding, then break 6 eggs into the pan. Pop the yolk of each egg lightly with the end of a wooden spoon and continue to stir gently until you have the desired consistency. The trick to eating them the way you like is to immediately take them out of the pan when they are done; if left in they will continue to cook in any residual heat.

Being posh with scrambled eggs. The classic way to enhance the scrambled egg experience is, of course, with smoked salmon, but try them with:

asparagus cooked until just tender and either served alongside or chopped and folded into the eggs as they are cooking;

slices of good ripe tomatoes, roughly chopped parsley and grated Parmesan, again folded into the eggs just before they are ready;

good-quality smoked bacon, fried in advance until crispy, cut into little strips (lardons) then folded in to the nearly finished eggs.

Fried eggs and chard. **This is a lovely brunch dish, inspired in part by the wonderful Pizza Fiorentino, the centre of which is dominated by a runny egg. For this dish I serve a mound of chard on a thick slice of toast (a sourdough bread is perfect, but don't go mad looking for some) topped with the fried egg. To give a further nod to the original pizza you can embellish the whole thing with grated Parmesan (in fact, any hard, crumbly cheese will do the trick). If you cannot get hold of chard, spinach is just as good. Take note that spinach will cook in about a third of the time that chard takes.**

For 4 people you need:

4 hefty handfuls of chard (approx. 900g/2lb), washed
2 tbsp olive oil
2 cloves garlic, crushed
1 tbsp red wine vinegar, or the juice of 1 lemon
a generous pinch of salt
4 freshly fried eggs
4 slices of toast
50g/2oz freshly grated Parmesan cheese

Separate the leaves of the chard from the stalks and cut the stalks into bite-sized pieces. Tear or cut the leaves into strips.

Heat the olive oil gently and throw in the garlic cloves. When they have begun to turn golden and soft, throw in the stalks and the vinegar or lemon juice. Add the salt and stir once. Cover and leave to steam for about 10 minutes.

When the stalks have softened add the leaves, stir once more and cover again. The leaves will be ready in just under 5 minutes or so, enough time for you to fry the eggs. The whole lot is ready to go on the toast when the eggs are done to your liking. I recommend that you leave the yolks as soft as you can since they form a kind of dressing for the greens when they ooze out all over the place. Serve with the Parmesan cheese at the table, and good strong coffee. This meal is a great way of atoning (only ever so slightly) for a night of over-indulgence.

Eggy bread. **Americans call this French toast. The reason may be the old French pudding 'Pain Perdu', in which stale brioche was impregnated with beaten egg and then fried in clarified butter. Children always seem to love this for breakfast. It can be sweet or savoury. Sprinkling the finished eggy bread with sugar and cinnamon is always popular, although many people enjoy it plain with obscene amounts of ketchup or brown sauce. To go all-out American you can serve French toast with maple syrup and grilled bacon, a slightly bizarre but famous pairing. Trust me, it works. In the summertime try Eggy bread with fresh fruit like strawberries or blueberries – delicious when macerated with lemon and sugar.**

For 4 people you need:

5 eggs, beaten
2 tbsp milk
a pinch of salt
butter
4 slices of white bread

Beat the eggs, milk and salt together in a bowl large enough for a slice of bread. Gently heat a knob of butter in a frying pan, so that it does not brown. When the pan is hot enough dip a slice of the bread in the egg mixture, coat both sides well and transfer to the pan. Fry for about 2 minutes on each side until golden and slightly crunchy.

Poached eggs. **A poached egg is a wonderful thing, well worth the extra effort involved. People are spooked by making them, but with fresh eggs and a little attention to detail they are easy. They are also very quick. To cook for any more than a couple of people, without stress, do them in batches of two.**

You need a decent-sized pan, about a third full of water. To the water add just a dash of vinegar and a generous pinch of salt.

When the water has reached simmering point lower the heat so that it will not come to the boil.

Break in the eggs. I do no more than two at a time since they are easier to fish out that way. If you are concerned with aesthetics you may make a gentle whirlpool in the middle of the pan just before you break in the eggs, since this will bully them into a neat shape. Do not let the water boil while you cook the eggs as this will cause them to break up.

A good poached egg with a runny middle and a 'pillow' of a white takes 3 minutes. Lift out with a slotted spoon and let the egg drain of excess liquid before serving, especially if you are having them on toast. Toast and water: Ugh.

A kipper and an egg? **If you are wondering about the question mark, it implies incredulity. Just as Lady Bracknell cries, 'A handbag?' in *The Importance of Being Earnest*, you must describe this meal as 'a kipper *and an egg?*'**

This is one of the most delicious breakfasts you can eat, but to the horribly grumpy owner of the worst bed and breakfast in Wales it was too horrific to even contemplate. I was with a friend who ate no meat, only fish. You could have bacon and sausages with your eggs, but not, it would seem, a kipper. I hasten to add that we did not make a fuss. There was sniggering and nothing more.

That day the best way in the world to get children to eat smoked fish for breakfast was born. The hammier you are with the acting, the more likely they are to tuck in.

You can do all this in one pan. Poach the kipper first; it takes about 6 minutes with the lid on. Don't let it boil or it could break up, just keep the water at a gentle simmer. Now pop it on a plate with a knob of butter to melt all over it. Ready the water for the egg with a shake of vinegar and follow the poaching method (see above). By the time the egg is ready you will have perfectly melted butter all over the kipper, and a lovely runny yolk. Crusty brown bread rather than toast is the perfect partner. This also makes a great lunch or even a starter. Serve it with a fresh, peppery watercress salad.

Mary's eggs. **This is the favourite childhood supper of a friend from Scotland. Mary is his mother's name and for as long as I have known him we have called this Mary's eggs. It is, in fact, her version of baked (or shirred) eggs. There was no written recipe. If Mary reads this I hope she will forgive my bungling attempts to do it justice.**

For 4 people you need:

butter for coating

1 ripe tomato, thinly sliced

a handful of chopped parsley

4 eggs

100g/3½oz grated crumbly cheese (Lancashire or Cheshire is best)

salt and pepper

Preheat the oven. You should have it on full whack – i.e. 250°C/475°F/ gas 9.

Coat 4 ramekins very generously with butter. Place a slice of the tomato in the bottom of each one and add a good pinch of parsley.

Break an egg into each ramekin and sprinkle on an equal amount of cheese. Season with a pinch each of salt and pepper.

Place the ramekins on a baking tray. If you want slightly soft yolks cook for 8 minutes. Add an extra 2 minutes if you don't. You can check that the eggs beneath the cheese are cooked through with a gentle prod, but not a knife or skewer. They should yield only slightly.

You can serve the eggs in the ramekins or, if you are feeling adventurous, turn them out. I quite like the surprise of finding soft yolk and then the tomato in the dish so I leave them in. However, you can use this recipe as a starter for a dinner party and turning out the eggs looks cute. You can do this even with the soft yolk if you are gentle. Run a knife round the edge of the ramekin, invert it over the plate you want to eat it off and tap the bottom of the ramekin lightly with a knife. Let gravity do the rest so count to twenty or something before peeking. For a richer meal you can add a tablespoon of soured cream to each egg.

Canapé. **(Illustrated) This is the snack to end all snacks. Birthday parties back in the seventies would have ended in a riot without it. I don't know whose mother did it first, but I like to think mine dreamed it up. I daren't ask now. It would be worse than discovering the truth about Santa if she revealed that it was a 'serving suggestion' or something.**

You need Ritz crackers. No other will do. Besides that indefinable Ritz taste, no other cracker is the right shape. You'll see what I mean, because this looks elegant in a sort of seventies way, as if the ingredients were meant for each other (they are). Basically, you are going to tower slices of hard-boiled egg and tomato on top of a cracker. Two alternating slices of each are ideal, go any higher and things look a bit 'Scooby Doo'. Only use the flat slices. No roof of egg, no end of tomato.

Scotch eggs. **My grandmother would never consider a picnic without her home-made Scotch eggs and yet she never wrote down her recipe.**

If locating a recipe resembling hers was hard, finding out why a Scotch egg is called a Scotch egg was even harder. I got nowhere. It occurred to me that the meat and aromatics mix for the eggs has a 'haggissy' feel to it, but I am clutching at Scotch straws, I think.

This recipe is adapted from one in the *The Prawn Cocktail Years* by Simon Hopkinson and Lindsey Bareham, an enjoyable book that takes a fond, but humorous look at how we used to eat out in the days before everything went all 'rocket and Parmesan shavings'.

If you don't fancy making your own mince, it is fine to get a butcher to make it for you. Good butchers will normally make mince on the lean side. For a decent Scotch egg mix you need some fattier cuts, so ask for a mince made from the shoulder and the belly. My butcher is happy to do that, so yours should be. If in doubt, ring ahead.

To make 10 scotch eggs you need:

2 eggs, beaten

400g/14oz semi-lean mince (or, if you want to do your own: 200g/7oz skinned, boned belly and 150g/5oz boned, lean shoulder meat; 75g/3oz bacon without rind and 50g/2oz pork fat)

grated zest of 1 lemon

1 tsp freshly ground black pepper

1 level tsp salt

3 sprigs of thyme leaves, off the twiggy bit and chopped

1 tbsp chopped parsley

6 sage leaves, chopped

250g/9oz fresh breadcrumbs

flour for dusting

oil for frying (don't use olive oil)

Put the eggs in cold water and bring to the boil. Cook for 4 minutes, then leave the eggs under running cold water for a further 3 minutes. Peel carefully and put to one side.

Mix the mince and all the flavourings in a large bowl until everything is amalgamated. The best way to do this is to use your hands, so please don't be squeamish about it. You're going to have to get mince all over your hands to do the eggs anyway.

Now set up your very own production line. Have 3 small bowls handy: one for the beaten eggs, one for the breadcrumbs and the last half-filled with flour. Roll all the hard-boiled eggs in the flour, shake off any excess and set aside.

To coat the eggs in mince, dust your hands with flour and pick up about 50g/2oz of mince (the equivalent of a heaped tablespoon). Flatten the mince in your right hand with your left, grab an egg and bring the mince around it, making sure it is fully encased. Do this with all the eggs.

Now dip each Scotch egg in flour, then egg, then breadcrumbs.

You really need to deep-fry these, so set a fryer to 160°C/325°F or fill a saucepan no more than a third full with the oil. Place over a medium heat for about 5 minutes (don't wander away from this kind of pan, ever). Test the oil by dropping in a scrap of bread. If it turns gold in less than 2 minutes the heat is right. Immerse the eggs in batches of 3 (less if the pan is small) and cook for about 8 minutes until crisp and golden. Transfer them onto kitchen paper to remove excess oil and serve warm or cold.

A bacon and egg pie (or is it a quiche?). **A ridiculous joke in the eighties used to run something along the lines of: 'Real men don't eat quiche, just bacon and egg pie'. Quite what was so emasculating about quiche has always eluded me. I think the joke bought into the idea that French food was fancy whilst British food was rough and ready. Ironically, quiche is neither fancy nor particularly French. Quiche comes from the German word *Kuchen* (meaning Kitchen but normally hinting at some kind of cake or flan). Lorraine refers to the region of Alsace and Lorraine and is not, as I once assumed, a person like the Suzette of crepes fame.**

So what exactly is the recipe below? Probably a quiche (sorry lads). But not quiche Lorraine, since I like mine with onions. You can modify the basic version any way you like. Smoked salmon instead of bacon is tasty and means you can skip including meat. My favourite meat-free version follows this one.

For a 20.5cm/8in tart case you need:

250g/9oz short crust pastry

4 eggs plus one extra to glaze the pastry

2 tbsp olive oil

1 onion, peeled and sliced

½ tsp salt

100g/3½oz good quality bacon (I use pancetta as it has less water content than other bacon)

200ml/7fl oz crème fraiche or soured cream

a sprig of thyme, leaves pulled off the twiggy bit

salt and pepper

Line the tart case with the pastry and rest it in the fridge for about 15 minutes. Preheat the oven to 200°C/400°F/mark 6 and pop in a baking tray or sheet larger than the base of the tart shell. If the oven and the tray are hot, and if you have rested the pastry, I promise that you won't need to blind bake this pastry. Just prick the base in a few spots with a fork and pop it in the oven for 10 minutes. Don't peek at it until then unless you can do it without opening the oven door (because pastry likes a constant temperature). After 10 minutes, glaze it with the spare egg (this bit isn't actually compulsory but it does give a barrier between pastry and filling). Cook the base for another 5 minutes and then rest it on a cooling rack.

Turn the oven down to 160°C/360°F/mark 3

Heat the oil in a frying pan and gently fry the onions with ½ teaspoon of salt. Give them at least 10 minutes but try not to let them brown. Add the bacon and fry for a further 5 minutes. Remove from the heat and transfer to a mixing bowl. Now break in the eggs. I don't beat them first and I don't do much more than run them around the bowl with the bacon and onions, making sure the yolks are broken. It adds texture to the pie. Now fold in the crème fraiche and the thyme. Season again to taste – about ½ teaspoon of salt and a very scant pinch of pepper should be fine.

You can now fill the tart case. Bake it for 15 minutes then check to see whether it has cooked. It may take anything from 15–25 minutes depending on how fierce your oven is and how cold the eggs were. When ready it will have set (basically it no longer wobbles) and will have browned ever so slightly on top. It's lovely cold, but if you're wrapping it to take out then make sure it is fully cooled before you do. Warm pastry will steam itself a little when confined, and can go a bit soggy.

'Green' quiche. **If this heading makes you think of Dr Zeuss's Green eggs and ham ('I do not like them Sam I am!') try to forget about it and read on... ! The main problem with vegetarian quiches is not, as some would have it, the lack of bacon (ha ha ha) but the wrong vegetables. Some may disagree but broccoli is the usual suspect in this regard because it 'sogs'. Spinach is another culprit. You don't really want anything that is going to add moisture to the eggs and soured cream. By all means use spinach if you are happy to blanch or sauté it then wring out all the excess liquid, but alternatively try this version with delicious, cheap spring greens.**

Follow the exact method for Bacon and Egg Pie (you can even leave the bacon in if you eat meat). Fry the onions, and while they are doing their thing, rip the leaves off two average sized heads of spring greens or Brussels tops. You want to end up with no stalk at all and two heads that yield about 100g/3½oz of leaf in raw form. If this seems a little wasteful just cast your mind back to how ludicrously cheap the vegetables were when you bought them. Now cut the leaves into strips and fry them with the onions for about 5 minutes. There should be no liquid at all from the greens but if there is, simply toss the mix around a colander for a few seconds before adding the eggs, cream and seasoning. Cook as specified in the recipe opposite. You will get some crispy greens at the top of the filling. They are delicious.

Mushroom quiche. **Mushrooms are a fine addition to a veggie quiche, and can also produce juices when fried. I personally go for oyster mushrooms or a mix of the wild kinds because they fry wonderfully and stay fairly dry. They are a little pricey but the 100g/3½oz that you need is not going to cost too much.**

Unlike the two methods above, I fry the mushrooms on a high heat, with the tiniest splash of oil, before cooking the onions on their own. You can fry the mushrooms very briskly, and in fact they take on a great character if allowed to catch slightly. If you want to use field mushrooms, 3 or 4 of the largest kind, thinly sliced, will taste lovely. Fry them with the almost finished onions for about 2 minutes (just long enough to wilt them) but you must throw them into a colander to remove the juices before adding the eggs.

A slice of toast. The Brits are said to be the world's most enthusiastic sandwich eaters. You could also say that what we don't stick between two pieces of bread we might try and smear over one piece of toast. Toast is the vehicle that can turn anything into a hand-held meal, from a fine piece of cheese to yesterday's shepherd's pie.

What was once almost certainly a way of making stale bread more palatable has become so beloved that no kitchen is complete without one particular gadget: the pop-up toaster, invented just after the First World War. At the time it must have seemed like the best thing since sliced bread.

The Romans bought leavened bread to these shores. 'Toast' comes from the Latin word *tostum* meaning 'to scorch' and drying bread out in front of a fire was one way to stop it going mouldy too quickly. But the British love affair with shoving all manner of food onto grilled bread may stem from a later era when people ate from 'trenchers'. These were baked, edible discs of wheat flour that could hold food. Thus, plates and cutlery were not needed. When the contents of the trencher were gone it was eaten too, no doubt impregnated with juices and flavours from the food it had held.

You'd be right if you imagined that the trencher was a sort of medieval (albeit less jolly version of) pizza, and look how popular that is today. Could it be that pizza reminds us of something more Olde Worlde than all that mozzarella and basil?

Another, more recently adopted, Italian import is bruschetta, which is stale, grilled bread rubbed with garlic and impregnated with olive oil. Slightly less well known, but equally delicious, is the Spanish equivalent, Pan Con Tomate (similar to bruschetta, but with the cut side of a tomato rubbed onto the bread so that it catches the juices). It seems that whenever the British take to a foreign food they soon sniff out the closest thing to toast on the menu and order it by the truckload. When was the last time you contemplated a curry without 'naan', grilled on the side of a fiercely hot tandoor oven?

In this chapter I hope to give you some fine recipes for embellishing the most humble slice of bread. Real toast fanatics should also check out the website: homagetotoast.co.uk, and the accompanying book *Toast: Homage to a Super Food*. It's an intriguing and often amusing read. The author, Nick Parker, starts by pointing out that no cookbook has ever devoted much time to toast. I hope, if he is reading, that he will be pleased to see it well represented here.

Baked field mushrooms. (Illustrated) Nature has a wonderful knack of producing the odd ingredient that can take as little or as much preparation as you care to devote your time to. Parasol-shaped field mushrooms are a prime example. Field mushrooms on toast make a great breakfast at any time of the year. Allow 3 or 4 of the larger black types per person, or simply buy enough to fill whatever size of baking dish you have. You can keep what you don't eat for a great addition to a salad or a sandwich later.

Preheat the oven to its highest setting – i.e. 250°C/475°F/gas 9. Pack the mushrooms fairly tightly in the baking dish, squeeze the juice of a lemon over and dot the tops of each mushroom with a small piece of butter (or drizzle them with olive oil instead). Sprinkle them generously with salt and, just before you pop them in the oven, run your hand under a cold tap and shake your hands dry over the mushrooms so that they get a splash of water.

Cover them with foil and bake for about 20 minutes. You can serve them just as they are, on toast, or with bacon and eggs for a real feast.

Roast tomatoes. I make no apologies here for cribbing my old boss David Eyre's unbeatable way of slow-roasting tomatoes in the oven until they are almost dried. As with the mushroom dish above I would urge you to eye up your favourite baking tray and pop out to buy as many good ripe tomatoes as it takes to fill it. Once roasted the tomatoes can be kept in olive oil for a few days and added to salads, sandwiches or pasta dishes. They are a wonderful accompaniment to grilled sardines or anchovies.

Preheat the oven to 120°C/250°F/gas 1/2.

Halve each tomato lengthways and scoop out the seeds with your fingers or a teaspoon. Line them up in the baking tray with a good drizzle of olive oil. Sprinkle them with salt and a very scant amount of sugar (this won't really sweeten them; it just eggs them on a bit). You can add a herb like thyme or oregano if you like.

Roast them, uncovered, for about 3 hours until they look, as David puts it, ugly. You will know what he means when you see them. Smash some onto a piece of toast whilst still warm for a real taste of summer.

'Real beans'. **Far from an attack on the ever-popular baked bean, which I adore, this is a more Mediterranean version using borlotti or canellini beans. It is essentially a warm salad and makes a fine summery lunch on a piece of toast made in the bruschetta style (see page 23). Come the early autumn, good greengrocers might have the brightly coloured, new season borlotti. They are unmistakable in their psychedelic pods, and inside they look like tiny speckled easter eggs. You need to buy about 1kg/2¼lb and shell them yourself. For this dish, out of season, I buy tinned borlotti. There are excellent brands available and they are often organic these days. The cooking and canning process makes them less starchy than the dried version, and of course you don't need to soak them overnight.**

For 4 people you need:

400g tin borlotti or canellini beans (drained weight is 240g/8½oz)

1 red onion, finely chopped

3 ripe tomatoes, skinned, deseeded and finely chopped

4 tbsp extra virgin olive oil

juice of 1 lemon

salt and pepper to taste

a handful of basil or parsley, roughly chopped

4 large slices (cut lengthways) of good country style bread, grilled and rubbed with a cut clove of garlic

a scant grating of Parmesan cheese (optional)

A wok is perfect for the quick cooking of the beans. You simply drain them of nearly all their stock, throw them in the wok with the onion, tomatoes, oil, lemon juice and seasoning and warm them through for a couple of minutes.

Remove the wok from the heat and throw in the herbs. Leave to rest for another couple of minutes while you deal with the bread. Top the grilled bread with the beans and, if you are including the cheese, grate it over the top of the finished dish. Serve with extra cheese and more oil if you wish.

This is great barbecue fare, by the way. I like to serve it with grilled sausages and a leafy salad. The sausages and bread can share the grill.

Broccoli and anchovy.

As odd as this combination sounds it is quite a classic. Traditionally it calls for the purple sprouting broccoli that appears around the end of February. You can actually use any greens you like, blanched and tossed, whilst still warm, in the dressing below. Although greens are delicious on toast and butter, Italian-style bruschetta has the edge in this case.

Trish Hilferty, of the Fox Dining Room in London, taught me how to make this. Be warned, it is addictive. You can spread it on toast all by itself. The amounts Trish gives below make a fair amount of the sauce, but it will keep for at least 2 or 3 weeks in the fridge.

You need:

150g tin cured anchovy fillets in oil

1 tbsp capers

2 cloves garlic

1 small red chilli, deseeded and chopped, or ½ tsp freshly ground black pepper

1 tbsp Dijon mustard

1 tbsp wine or sherry vinegar

350ml/12fl oz olive oil (preferably a pomace and not extra virgin)

A food processor is ideal for this. Blitz the anchovies, capers, garlic, chilli or pepper, mustard and vinegar to a paste, then slowly start to add the oil. You will end up with a stiff mayonnaise-type sauce. There is the outside chance that it will split and become more like vinaigrette, but don't tear your hair out, it still tastes good.

Add quite a conservative amount to the greens when you toss them and give people the option of adding more at the table. Serve on buttered toast or bruschetta.

Creamed kidneys.

This is a wonderful brunch-type dish of lamb's kidneys in a béchamel-style sauce.

For 4 people you need:

1 tbsp olive oil

500g/1lb 2oz lambs' kidneys, washed and stripped of the suet (the fat that sometimes encases them)

1 tbsp butter

1 tbsp plain flour

200ml/7fl oz milk

1 tsp salt

a generous pinch of freshly ground black pepper

Heat the oil in a medium-sized saucepan and fry the kidneys, quite hard, for about 10 minutes, turning occasionally. Remove them from the pan and set aside.

Add the butter to the pan and return it to the heat. Add the flour and, using a wooden spoon, stir it briskly into the hot butter. When it has been absorbed (don't worry if it looks a bit lumpy) add the milk and seasoning. Stir vigorously until the milk begins to thicken and any lumps have melted away. Return the kidneys to the pan with any juices they have made. Simmer for a couple more minutes and serve on thickly sliced, buttered toast.

Potted shrimps. No finer topping for a slice of toast exists, if you ask me. Finding the shrimps to make this from scratch is a little tricky. In good fishmongers you may come across them already potted, which will be fine.

Little has changed in this industry since it began in the eighteenth century although the fishermen who harvested the shrimps by horse and cart back then might be surprised to see tractors doing the job today. The tiny brown shrimps (Morecambe Bay in Lancashire is most famous for them) are what you need. They are fished in the vast stretches of sand and mud banks exposed by low tides and boiled in sea water before being shelled. Obviously, potting the shrimps was a way to increase their shelf life in the days before refrigeration, but something about the delicate spicing of the butter and the salty closeness of the fish makes this taste very special, as if the shrimps, mace and butter were made for each other.

For 500g/1lb 2oz of shrimps you need:

125g/4oz unsalted butter (remember the shrimps were cooked in brine)

a pinch of mace

a pinch of cayenne pepper (I sometimes use a shake of Tabasco sauce instead)

¼ nutmeg, grated

You will need to clarify the butter, but it is pretty straightforward. Heat the butter gently in a saucepan and let it simmer for at least 10 minutes. After that, watch it like a hawk. The milk solids, that first show themselves as white flecking, will start to go a golden brown colour. This can happen fairly quickly if the water:fat ratio of the butter is low. As soon as you see the flecks turn darker, strain the butter through two layers of kitchen towel and reserve about one-third of it, keeping it warm so that it doesn't set.

Return the rest to the heat with the shrimps and spices. Simmer for about 5 minutes and pot in ramekins. You then cover the potted shrimps with a little of the reserved butter to preserve them for longer. They will keep for up to one week in the fridge.

I like to spread the potted shrimps on toast (cold) but they are equally delicious warmed up and served with brown bread.

Crab. **The brown meat (the bit that looks scary, but tastes the best) is one of nature's ready-made pâtés. A good fishmonger will have dressed crabs, but you will find the taste of your own cooked crab is an experience not to be missed.**

Cooking a crab is not a job for the squeamish. To ensure that the crab is fresh and safe to eat you must make sure it is alive when you buy it. You will have to kill it yourself, just before you cook it. It is not true that you have to boil the crab alive. You should turn it onto its back and lift the ribbed flap of shell (it's very obvious). Using a skewer and a hammer you spear the crab in the softer area beneath the flap. It will die instantly.

Crab needs to be put into rapidly boiling, very salty water (some people say you should salt the water heavily enough for an egg to float in it, but I just taste it to see if it is like the sea). If the crab is 500g/1lb 2oz it should boil for 15 minutes. If the crab is closer to 1kg/2¼lb it needs 20 minutes (basically add 5 minutes per 500g in weight).

Allow the crab to cool once cooked and lay it on its back again. Pull off the legs and claws and set them aside. Now work around the edge of the protruding section of shell with a small knife and lift it off the crab. You can now see the inedible gills, which you remove and throw away. They are grey and slightly furry and have the apt nickname of 'dead man's fingers', which makes them very easy to spot.

The rest of the crab is edible. I use a nutcracker to break open the claws for white meat and a skewer to get at the bits hidden in crevices. The brown meat is easily scooped out with a spoon. The white meat can be potted in a similar way to shrimps (see opposite), but I think it is even better just eaten off the claw as you get to it. A whole crab, with toast and butter, is an amazing meal. Simply spread the brown meat on toast like a pâté and eat the white with your fingers.

Mackerel. In a minute I will give you my mother's recipe for smoked mackerel pâté, but I should also tell you that I grew up eating fresh mackerel on toast for breakfast. In the summer my uncle would go mackerel fishing in Cardigan Bay. This was invariably early in the mornings so that when he returned with a huge catch my grandmother would fillet a couple of the fish and fry them with a little butter. This is a great breakfast for a weekend. Grab really fresh mackerel. There is no point in me telling you how many fish to buy because mackerel (truly one of our finest wild foods) vary greatly in size. You must do this at a fishmongers (don't buy it shrink-wrapped): get the fishmonger to fillet the fish for you. Season each fillet with a little flour, salt and pepper. Fry the fillet in butter for about 2 minutes on each side and serve with lemon and parsley.

Smoked mackerel pâté.

A fine spread for toast. My mother always adds horseradish to hers, but you can do it without.

The fillets are usually sold in pairs so for 2 fillets you need:

1 tbsp freshly grated horseradish (optional)

1 tbsp soft, unsalted butter

100g/3½oz crème fraîche, or Greek yoghurt

juice of 1 lemon

salt and pepper to taste

If you can get hold of fresh horseradish (it looks like a very misshapen parsnip with a brown skin) cut off a small section and peel it. Grate it standing near an open window because it is very strong. Good for the sinuses!

A food processor is perfect for smoked mackerel pâté. Pull the skin off the fillets (you can do this with your hands) and flake the meat. Whiz up with all the ingredients until you have a spreadable paste. It will keep in the fridge for days. Serve on hot, buttered toast.

Soft roes.

Herring roe is best for toast, and it is probably what you are most likely to find at the fishmonger's. Weight is not the best guideline here. Tell him or her how many people you are feeding and you can both visually judge the quantity of roe.

Season a couple of tablespoons of plain flour with salt and pepper. Toss the roes in the flour. Heat a frying pan with butter and, when bubbling, fry the roe for about 1 minute on each side. You should serve the roe on toast with parsley and lemon.

Glamorgan sausages. The 'meat' in a Glamorgan sausage is like the 'rabbit' in a Welsh rabbit (see page 35). In a Glamorgan sausage, the bread and cheese are bound together with finely chopped leeks, before being shaped into patties for frying. They are delicious morsels and for many years now I've included them in my Christmas dinners, as a spin on the old chipolata theme. They are easy to make, please vegetarians and carnivores alike, and children love them. Try them with some roast red onions or even a tin of baked beans (anyone who has fallen for the charm of beans and cheese on toast will know what I am saying here).

For authenticity you need a crumbly cheese, Caerphilly being the best. A good Lancashire will also do the trick but I have resorted to cheddar before without disastrous results. I also tend to stray from the traditional use of mustard powder, preferring a dollop of wholegrain, as I think it is great with leeks. I include both options below.

For 4 people you need:

3 slices of white bread, crusts removed

2 finely chopped leeks

a handful of chopped parsley

200g/7oz grated Caerphilly or Lancashire cheese

1 tsp wholegrain mustard or a pinch of mustard powder

salt and freshly ground black pepper to taste

3 eggs

The bread is best 'pulsed' in a food processor, but it can be shredded (mind your fingers) on the largest blade of a cheese grater. Tip it into a large bowl with the leeks, parsely, cheese, mustard, salt and pepper.

Add two of the eggs, beaten, and mix thoroughly. You should be able to roll the mixture into small sausage shapes. Dip them into the remaining egg, then the breadcrumbs. They are now ready for shallow frying or grilling, until golden brown outside and gooey with the cheese within (they take approximately 7 minutes). Serve immediately.

Chicken livers.

You can make chicken livers into a fine pâté, as I will show you, but you can also eat the seared livers on toast for a pretty hearty, quick meal. Chicken livers are very cheap. You should make sure that they come from a free-range bird.

For a light lunch for 4 people you need:

1 tbsp olive oil

200g/7oz chicken livers, washed, with the gristle removed

1 tbsp butter

2 cloves garlic, sliced

4 or 5 sage leaves, left whole

1 tbsp balsamic vinegar

a pinch each of salt and freshly ground black pepper

4 slices hot, buttered toast

Heat a large frying pan with the oil. Fry the chicken livers for about 2 minutes on each side. You want them to caramelize a bit on the surfaces. Tip the cooked livers into a small bowl and set aside.

Return the pan to the heat and add the butter. As soon as it starts to fizz add the garlic and sage leaves. Literally move them around the pan for just under a minute and then add the vinegar. Remove the pan from the heat immediately and pour the contents over the livers. Shake the bowl gently to coat the livers in the dressing. Season with the salt and pepper and pop them onto the toast.

Chicken liver pâté.

This is probably the fastest meat pâté you can make. It is rich and creamy. The quantities below will serve up to 6 people, but it keeps well in the fridge.

For 6 people you need:

150g/5oz unsalted butter

1 tbsp olive oil

200g/7oz chicken livers, washed, with the gristle removed

3 or 4 sage leaves, chopped

2 cloves garlic, sliced

2 tbsp cooking brandy

2 level tsp English mustard powder

¼ nutmeg, grated

1 tsp salt

a pinch of freshly ground black pepper (optional)

First, clarify the butter following the method for potted shrimps (see page 28). Reserve about one-third in a small bowl, keeping it warm so that it doesn't set.

Heat a large frying pan and add the remaining butter with the olive oil. Fry the chicken livers, sage and garlic over a gentle heat for about 5 minutes, turning them over halfway through the cooking time. Remove them from the pan and set aside.

Return the pan to the heat and pour in the brandy. Remove from the heat immediately and swirl the brandy around the pan to mop up the juices. Pour it over the chicken livers.

Put all the cooked ingredients with the mustard, nutmeg, salt and pepper into a food processor and pulse until you have a paste. Press the paste into a small container and cover it with the reserved butter. Refrigerate, preferably overnight to let it set. It will still be very spreadable. Serve with hot toast (you can use the butter on top of the pâté to spread on the toast).

Welsh rabbit **(or is it rarebit?).** **When Jane Grigson wrote *English Food* she called Welsh rarebit a 'false etymological refinement'. I think she meant that the dish had been renamed by people with a sense of humour failure. Welsh rabbit (as mentioned in journals as long ago as 1725) is like Scotch woodcock or Bombay duck. It is not what you think. If the title misleads then so do the ingredients, for a Welsh rabbit is much more than the sum of its parts (cheese on toast). In the days before café lattes and panini it was a standard in tearooms all over the land.**

The crumblier the cheese you use, the better. I particularly like Cheshire or Lancashire. If you can source good Caerphilly, then you are in for an even more authentic treat.

The recipe that follows is the one I grew up with, but I owe the addition of Worcestershire sauce to a friend.

For 4 people you need:

250g/9oz grated cheese (see above)

6 tbsp beer, or Guinness

1 tbsp butter

1 tbsp wholegrain mustard

a splash of Worcestershire sauce

4 slices bread for toasting: white or brown, but nothing fancy

a bag of plain flour, standing by

Gently heat the cheese, beer and butter over a low flame, until it begins to go creamy. Add the mustard and Worcestershire Sauce. On occasion, things may look a little curdled, as if the cheese and beer did not want to come together. If it bothers you (and it has no effect on the flavour) you may add a teaspoon of flour to help the ingredients become a paste.

Allow the paste to cool. It will now resemble a slightly fibrous paste. In fact there is something about it sometimes that looks 'rabbity', although that may be my imagination.

Heat a grill and start to toast the bread on both sides. When it is ready, lay the toast on a tray or grill pan and spread it with a generous amount of the paste. Return to the grill and cook until the topping is golden brown.
Eat immediately.

Regional variations. English rabbit is grilled cheese on bread that has been impregnated with red wine.

Scotch rabbit is grilled cheese on buttered toast.

Wales wins.

A ploughman's lunch. If you find yourself with good cheeses and fresh bread the last thing you want to do is grill either of them. I find that a home-made ploughman's makes a great lunch. A really good ploughman's needs an apple and at least one or two pickles. The two recipes below are the kind that you can 'rustle up'. Neither needs to be made in advance although they can be stored. They will complement a plate of cold meats as well.

Pickled gooseberries.

An unusual treatment for gooseberries that I now make in bulk every summer. The fruit will be good enough to eat within a couple of hours, but put some aside for Christmas. Amazingly the gooseberries stay crunchy like a zingy little pickled onion.

For 1 large jar you need:

1kg/2½lb gooseberries, hulled, but left whole

1 litre/1¾pt white wine vinegar

1 level tsp salt

250g/9oz sugar

3 or 4 black peppercorns

Heat the vinegar with the salt, sugar and peppercorns and simmer until the sugar has dissolved. Add the gooseberries and remove from the heat. Allow to cool completely before eating any. If storing, keep in jars in a cool dark place.

Instant pickles.

This method of pickling is one I picked up in Indonesia, where most meals include some sort of cured fruit or vegetable ('achar'). Not only is it incredibly easy, it can look stunning if you mix and match ingredients. The trick is to slice them as finely as you can. The mixture below is my favourite.

For 1 large jar you need:

1 red onion, finely sliced

1 bulb fennel, finely sliced

1 small cucumber, finely sliced

1 carrot, finely sliced

1 handful of radishes, finely sliced, or very finely sliced turnip

roughly ¼ cauliflower, in very small florets

50g/2oz salt

a handful of peppercorns or mustard seeds (optional)

The pickling:

500ml/17fl oz white wine (or rice wine) vinegar

250g/9oz caster sugar

1 level tbsp salt

¼ tsp turmeric

2 cloves

1 bay leaf

1 whole red chilli, slit lenthways (optional)

½ tsp whole coriander seeds or peppercorns (optional)

Put all the ingredients for the pickling in a pan with 500ml/17fl oz of water and simmer gently until the sugar has dissolved. Pour it over the vegetables and make sure they are immersed in the liquid.

By the time the mix has cooled the pickle is ready to eat. If you plan to store it for more than a day or so make sure you keep it in a jar in the fridge.

Three preserves. There is little point in me waxing lyrical about how toast and jam were made for each other. Everybody knows it. Nor am I going to start enthusing too much about making your own preserves because I'd be lying if I said it was something that I do with any regularity.

However, you will feel very good about yourself having made a jam or marmalade. For a start, the stuff you make at home will beat shop-bought versions hands down. Even if it doesn't look as pretty or set as uniformly, it will be jam as jam was intended – fruit preserved with sugar and nothing more. Making a preserve is also one of those ridiculously easy tasks that brings with it a sense of having achieved something quite profound... not only as you enjoy the mild thrill of plopping it into a warm jar, but every time you eat it. Which could go on for weeks!

What puts most of us off preserve-making? Probably the thought of buying and sterilizing jars, but almost certainly having nowhere to keep rows of marmalade. Few of us seem to have any kind of pantry any more. The following recipes are here to pass on my own, pretty slapdash attitude to making the few jams that I do get around to. I don't buy jars; I stash old ones when I've done with them. Perhaps I shouldn't admit this, but I currently have some marmalade lurking in a yoghurt pot. That is why all the quantities that follow will only require one average-sized jar. If you fancy making any of them in batches just multiply the quantities by whatever number of jars you have. This is pretty foolproof.

As for the actual recipes that follow, I've chosen the three preserves that disappoint me most when I buy (or in the case of gooseberry jam, can't find) them. None of them take long to make.

The average-sized jar these days seems to hold about 450g/1lb of jam so all the recipes will make roughly that amount.

Sterilizing. This really shouldn't present an issue if you are making preserves in small quantities like this. Since I have no larder I keep all my preserves in the fridge. I've never found mould growing on any of them. The best way to sterilize a jar is to wash it in hot soapy water, rinse it thoroughly and allow it to dry in an oven on 140–150°C/275–300°F/gas 1–2. Add the preserve to the jar whilst still hot and seal the jam beneath a disc of baking parchment to shield it from the lid.

Gooseberry jam.

We had this every summer when I was a boy. The gooseberry 'jams' exceptionally well and as a child I was always fascinated to see it turn from a murky green to a burnt orange colour. I'm including a recipe here not just because gooseberry jam is an easy one to make, but because it is hard to buy.

For one jar you need:
450g/1lb gooseberries, hulled
450g/1lb granulated sugar
juice of 1 lemon

Pour 200ml/7fl oz of water into a pan and add the gooseberries, sugar and lemon juice. Boil rapidly for about 10 minutes then simmer for a further 20 minutes. Test for setting point before you put it in the jar (for the saucer test see One-orange marmalade on page 39).

It's not a well known fact, but gooseberry jam is a formidable partner for Cheddar cheese. Do try it.

Lemon curd. **My Aunt Lori moved to Portugal and now grows lemons in her garden. This is a beautifully sharp version of lemon curd that she makes when the tree is laden with fruits. I have to make my own curd now because no shop, market stall, village fête or whatever has matched Aunty Lori's for its sheer lemonyness. And believe me, I've searched for one. Portugal is a long way to go for a slice of toast.**

You must hunt down some unwaxed lemons for this. Nearly all supermarkets offer them now. They do seem pricey compared to their shiny counterparts, but you're only buying 2 or 3 at the most, and you're using the zest (skin). Not only is it better to eat lemon curd without wax in it, it's easier to grate untreated zest. The amounts below will fill one decent-sized jar so double or treble up as you see fit. Lemon curd only keeps for a couple of weeks and you must store it in the fridge.

For one jar you need:

50g/2oz unsalted butter
2 large eggs
100g/3½oz caster sugar
grated zest and juice of 2 or 3 unwaxed lemons, depending on their size

Melt the butter gently and leave it to one side.

Beat the eggs and caster sugar in a mixing bowl until pale and smooth. Add the lemon zest and juice to the egg mix and whisk again. Now whisk in the melted butter.

You can cook this one of two ways. Either use a saucepan large enough to suspend the bowl over and fill two-thirds full of water, then bring to a boil, or cook the curd in a saucepan over a gentle heat. The saucepan must be heavy-bottomed and you need a fair amount of confidence for the second method. Either way, you cook the curd, stirring constantly with a wooden spoon, until it thickens considerably. In the bowl this can take up to 20 minutes. In the pan as little as 10 minutes.

The way to tell if it has got to setting point is to watch for the spoon starting to leave a trail as you stir. You will see what I mean. The trail will be faint and disappears quickly, but it's unmistakable. Chill the curd in a sterilized jar (see page 37) and leave it for a couple of hours minimum before eating.

When Seville oranges make their brief appearance in January you could try making orange curd following the method above. It's delicious, if slightly sweeter because the orange is bitter, but has less juice. This brings us neatly onto marmalade.

One-orange marmalade. **In 2002 the *Daily Telegraph* produced a fascinating cookbook based on readers' recipes called *It's Raining Plums*. Anyone keen on seasonal cookery should buy it. I was delighted to find that it contained this version of marmalade because it fits into the idea of making small amounts of preserves so well. Given that you need just an orange, a bag of sugar and some water it shouldn't have caused me too much pain to read that the marmalade is ideally made over three days. But of course it did, because I was so excited that I wanted to do it all in one go. You can, by the way, if you modify the recipe a little. My apologies to Mrs Jean Mackay of Leicester for mucking around with her marmalade.**

For one jar you need:
1 Seville orange
500g/1lb 2oz granulated sugar

Halve the orange and dig out the pips with a knife. Put them to one side. Now quarter the orange and slice it finely. Pour 500ml/17fl oz of water into a pan, add the orange slices and throw in the pips. Bring to the boil, then simmer for about 30 minutes. Fish out the pips with a spoon and throw them away.

Now add the sugar and return the pan to the heat to boil fairly rapidly for about 30 minutes, or until it reaches setting point. To test for setting point, chill a small plate or saucer in the freezer or ice compartment of a fridge for at least 10 minutes. Take it out and spoon a little of the marmalade onto the saucer. Return it to the freezer for about 2 minutes. Its behaviour will tell you where your marmalade is at. If it has gone wrinkly and slightly jelly-like, you're there. If not, continue cooking and test again.

One-orange marmalade is intensely orangey but pretty sweet, by the way. You can make it sharper by adding the juice of half a lemon to the water, or you can give it a kick with a very scant grating of ginger before you start to cook it.

A bowl of soup. The invention of soup is probably as old as the first cooking pot. The earliest soups (or potages) were literally broths produced by boiling meat and were spooned over bread or gruel made from cereals and pulses. These were meagre but filling meals for the poor. If you were lucky, or could afford it, the broth was followed by some of the meat from that pot. This is possibly why soup heralds the beginning of a meal to this day.

No matter how poorly or robust we feel, soup is usually just the ticket. How many of us actually make soup on a regular basis is open to question. There are definitely 'soup people'. Some folk seem to have been born with the confidence to fling open the barest of cupboards and improvise. Others find the whole thing a little long-winded or complicated and only attempt it when they feel duty bound to serve people more than one course at dinner.

I think I fall somewhere between the two. I've never worked in a kitchen that doesn't include soup on the menu. Sometimes I can't wait to get my head round the ins and outs of the soup pot and sometimes it feels like a chore. I eat a lot of soup, but I rarely buy it in. This is not out of snobbery, but I do know what I like (and what I don't like) to read in the ingredients list.

I don't like soups that have a ton of flour, or cornstarch, lurking in some gloopy suspension. A fine velouté or roux is a great way to start a soup, but, used wrongly, it is also a great way of skimping on other, more wholesome additions. Neither do I like soups that pretend to be exotic or otherworldly by assaulting you with too many herbs and spices. The worst culprits are dried oregano and black pepper. Less is definitely more when it comes to the flavour of a good soup. These two niggles rule out a lot of commercially produced varieties. There have been great improvements in several brands over the years, but old habits die hard. When I'm in the mood for soup I've got to make it at home.

This presents a lazybones like me with the challenge of breezing into my 'hearth-free' kitchen and emerging (less than several hours later) with a steaming bowlful of something marvellous. I might want my grandmother's cawl, but I lack both her patience and her Aga so over the years I've negotiated many a shortcut. I hope I can guide you through one or two and leave you with some of the (slightly smug) satisfaction the following recipes have given me.

The first and most significant shortcut I use may horrify some of you. You can ignore it of course.

Soup without stock (or black pepper). This may seem like sacrilege to some, but I very rarely make stock for soups. For once this is not down to sheer laziness. In fact, I was once lucky enough to work with an Italian called Carla Tomasi, who taught me to make soup without stock, and (in case you wonder why I mentioned it earlier) forbade the use of black pepper: 'That will be on the table if they want it,' she would say. 'Don't be a pepper bully.'

She was right. Black pepper will dominate the flavour of a soup unless it is used very judiciously. It is best served as a condiment. The only soup in this book containing black pepper is Mulligatawny, which needs it.

All soups in Carla's kitchen were made by cooking the bulky ingredients slowly with butter or olive oil and a dash of salt. Nothing more. The gentle frying and the inclusion of the salt leaches out juices and flavours from the ingredients and is known as 'sweating'. For every soup in this book I will prescribe sweating vegetables before you do anything else. Please try this method, as it does give unrivalled flavour and saves you a lot of effort.

Soups thickened without flour. Besides the odd nugget of pasta, rice or barley, the soups in this book thicken themselves. Roux, veloutés and white sauces do feature elsewhere and I do not intend to make you fearful of anything like that, but I do want to present soup-making as something that is incredibly easy.

I haven't even omitted flour deliberately; it's just that none of the soups I like need it. No flour, by sheer coincidence, also means less fat (since a roux needs butter or oil), so that even the creamiest recipes that follow can be eaten without guilt or angst. Neither will they upset an already delicate tummy, should you be considering a soup because you are under the weather.

A lot of soup in one go. The following recipes will all feed about 6 people. I am incapable of making small batches of soup and in the days before I owned a freezer I would end up living off the stuff for days at a time. Now I hoard plastic yoghurt pots. These are a handy size for freezing enough soup for 1 or 2 people to eat at a later stage. Make soup 'in bulk' and you will always have something to fall back on.

Soup with room to manoeuvre. The very nature of all the soups in this book means that, on the whole, there are few golden rules when it comes to making them. I do hope that you will not be put off trying any soups that follow because you can't find this or forgot to buy that. You may have stumbled upon a revelation. Where I have remembered to point them out there should be scope for even shorter shortcuts than the ones I usually stick to! Years of experimenting and improvising have gone into the soups of today. My cawl is not the last word in Welsh cuisine. A reader from Milan may laugh out loud at my bungling attempts to produce minestrone. By all means follow my advice on soup, but only as long as you feel you need to. As soon as you feel confident enough to go off this particular form of beaten track, do so!

We start our potted soup odyssey with meals in one bowl...

A meal in a bowl.

Cawl. **For me, Cawl (pronounced like 'vowel') is the ultimate meal in a bowl. There are probably as many recipes for this traditional Welsh soup as there are households in the Principality. I learned mine from my grandmother, who would invariably greet guests with huge, steaming bowls of the stuff. When I was young we lived in south Wales, and the journey north to my grandparents in Cardiganshire was (for a child) long and tortuous. This was the reward.**

You can use any cut of lamb for cawl. The cheaper the better! It was historically made with the leftover meat and juices of a pot roast. I have broken with my grandmother's tradition of using the breast over the years because I find that nothing makes a broth like a shank. I like to start the soup a day in advance. That way the excess fat can be effortlessly skimmed from the broth before it is added to the meat and vegetables.

For 6 people you need:

The meat:

3 shanks of lamb
1 whole, unpeeled onion
2 tomatoes (optional)
1 carrot
1 stick celery
3 tbsp vinegar
3 tbsp salt

The soup:

2 tbsp dripping or oil
2 onions, peeled and chopped
2 leeks, trimmed and chopped
2 carrots, diced
1 turnip, or potato, peeled and roughly diced
1 stick celery, chopped
100g/3½oz (or about 3 tbsp) red lentils
100g/3½oz (or about 3 tbsp) pearl barley
2 litres/3½pints (or thereabouts...whatever is left, really) of the broth
salt to taste

Put the lamb in a large saucepan with 4 litres/7 pints of water and add the onion, tomatoes (if using), carrot, celery, vinegar and salt. Simmer (but do not boil) this for about 3 hours, skimming occasionally to remove any scum that rises to the top of the liquid, until the meat is tender and nearly falling off the bone. Remove the meat and vegetables (you can discard the vegetables) and cool the resultant broth overnight. The next day the fat will be a thick hard lid, which you can remove and either keep as dripping or discard. The meat on the shank can also be trimmed of any unwanted fat (I actually don't bother), then pulled to bits, ready for the soup.

To make the soup, heat the dripping or oil in a large pan and gently sauté the onions, leeks, carrots, turnip or potato and celery.

When the vegetables are just getting tender add the lentils, pearl barley, the lamb and the broth. Cook for about 1½ hours, or until the broth has thickened, with the lentils just barely soft, but chewy. If it is all thickening to the point where you become alarmed do not worry, just add water and adjust the seasoning as you go. With all the flavours already in the pot you are in no real danger of a bland cawl. Chopped mint at the table makes a lovely addition, and of course you need good bread for mopping the bowl.

Scotch broth. Scotch broth and cawl are really regional variations of one another. To convert your cawl, substitute dried peas for the lentils and a similar quantity of chopped cabbage for the potatoes. Scotch broth is served differently to cawl in that it is added to a bowl of boiled potatoes.

Chicken and dumplings in broth.

Much has been written about the restorative qualities of chicken soup. Some people even believe it is a cure for the common cold. This is the most 'low maintenance' of all the soups in this section. Those who find themselves lacking time might be glad to know that the whole thing comes together very swiftly.

When it comes to buying the bird, do yourself a favour and go for a proper, free-range hen. An alternative to buying a whole bird is to make up a similar weight in joints like leg and thigh (which will give you the best stock). A couple of poussin (spring chickens) is also plenty.

You needn't bother making dumplings although I swear they are a breeze. If you really can't handle the idea, try using gnocchi or noodles. If you have cooked rice lying around that will also do the trick.

For 6 people you need:

The broth:

1½–2kg/3¼–4½lb free-range chicken
2 carrots
4 unpeeled cloves garlic
2 unpeeled onions
1 stick celery
3 bay leaves

The soup:

2 onions, peeled and chopped
3 cloves garlic, chopped
2 leeks, trimmed and thickly sliced
2 sticks celery
2 carrots, peeled and finely sliced
2 tbsp olive oil
2 litres/3½ pints of stock from the chicken
2 bay leaves
1 tbsp salt
1 tbsp Worcestershire sauce
1 tsp red wine vinegar
1 tsp sugar

The dumplings:

100g/3½oz self-raising flour
1 tsp salt
50g/2oz shredded suet, or cold butter

To make the broth, put the chicken, whole or otherwise, in a large pot with the carrots, garlic, onions, celery and bay leaves. Cover with about 4 litres/7 pints of water and bring to simmering point. Do not let it boil at any time. Remove the scum that appears on the surface of the stock. Cook the bird for about 1½ hours and check to see if it is ready. If a leg or wing comes away from the rest of the body with the gentlest of tugs it is done. Remove the chicken from the stock, allow it to cool, then pick the meat off the breast and legs in fairly substantial chunks (that is to say, as it falls into your hands). Strain the stock and discard the vegetables. You will have more broth than you need for the soup, but chicken stock is such a handy thing to have around that it is worth freezing what is left.

To make the soup, fry the onions, garlic, leeks, celery and carrots in the olive oil until they are just starting to wilt – about 10 minutes. Add the stock and bay leaves and simmer, without boiling, for around 30 minutes, or until the vegetables are really nice and tender. Add the cooked chicken meat. Now season the soup with the salt, Worcestershire sauce, vinegar and sugar. Simmer for another 15 minutes.

Whilst that is happening you have eons of time to make the dumplings. Rub the flour, salt and suet or butter together very briefly. Add 3 tablespoons of water, one tablespoon at a time, and knead lightly into a soft dough. Break it into about 16 small balls and pop them into the soup. They will probably sink, but will rise again very quickly. They are ready to eat after about 20 minutes.

Note that if you are making the soup a day or more in advance, don't add the dumplings until you are reheating to serve. They do not like to sit around in the broth.

Split pea and ham soup. **Something about this soup tastes as old as time. Like the Cawl or scotch broth, it is best made in two stages. I like to boil a ham hock (the shin) and use the resulting broth to make the soup. I add the meat from the hock at the end. However, you do not have to do it that way. The very nature of split peas and lentils means that they become flavoursome and nourishing pretty quickly. Two ways of making this soup follow.**

For 6 people you need:

a fairly small ham hock, preferably smoked. It will probably weigh from 750g–1kg/1lb 10oz–2¼lb

2 carrots, left whole

1 onion, unpeeled, cut in half

1 stick celery, whole, with the leaves if possible

2 cloves

1 bay leaf

500g/1lb 2oz split peas

Method 1 (for rustic, earthy types). Cook the hock in 1.4 litres/2½ pints of water with all the vegetables, the cloves and bay leaf. It needs to simmer but not boil. Skim away any scum that rises to the top of the broth. You need to cook this for about 3 hours, or until the meat is very tender. When it is done, remove it from the pot and set it aside in a cool place. Strain the stock and discard the vegetables. Chill the stock and the hock overnight.

The next day you should have a hock that is easy to pick into little bits (throw away the fatty bit, which looks like bacon rind). You will also have a stock that has turned to jelly. If there is a white film of fat on the top of it scrape it off. It's basically home-made lard so keep it if you want.

Heat the broth in a large pot and when it is simmering throw in the split peas. Cook for a couple of hours and check the progress of the peas. When they are soft and the whole thing starts to look thick and soupy, check the seasoning and add the meat. This is a winter lunch like no other.

For 6 people you need:

500g/1lb 2oz red or yellow lentils

1 clove

1 bay leaf

2 tbsp olive oil

1 large onion, chopped

1 stick celery, roughly chopped

1 carrot, peeled and diced

1 leek, trimmed and roughly chopped

250g/9oz good-quality streaky bacon, or cooked ham, roughly chopped

salt to taste

Method 2 (for urban, I can't be doing with all this 'day before' nonsense types). Put the lentils into a large pan with 1 litre/1¾ pints of water. Bring to a fairly rolling boil, but don't go anywhere. With a ladle at the ready, stand guard over the pot and skim any scum that rises to the surface. At first it may seem like a lot. If the water goes very frothy and looks like it may boil over, lower the heat. When you think you have got rid of all the scum, throw in the clove and the bay leaf but no other seasoning. Allow the lentils to simmer away, but keep an eye on them for any more of that scum. This should be easy because now it's time to fry the vegetables.

Heat the oil in another pan and gently fry the onion, celery, carrot and leek. After about 10 minutes, add the bacon or ham. Keep gently frying and stirring for another 10 minutes or so, on a very gentle heat, then add the whole lot to the lentils. Stir everything in and keep simmering until the lentils are falling apart and the whole thing is looking thick and soupy. This can take anything up to about 45 minutes. Check the seasoning (you are bound to need salt unless the bacon was very salty) and serve.

Minestrone. I think that if you asked most Brits to name a 'foreign' soup, they would say minestrone. It has been well and truly adopted. This also has to be the most abused soup on the planet. An unfortunate association exists between a packet and this soup. People think they don't like minestrone because of the awful industrial versions. It's actually almost impossible not to like the real thing.

Real minestrone (Italian, obviously) is in fact part of a family of 'big soups' (*minestra*). These soups vary from region to region but most contain a base of aromatic vegetables (onions, garlic, celery etc...) and possibly a legume or pulse (beans and peas). There may or may not be meat as well. It is the addition of pasta or rice that makes *minestra* become minestrone.

I must point out that here we will part ways with authenticity. There is little point telling you exactly how to make minestrone, since you might be put off if you can't get hold of one of the ingredients. It really is about using what is around. I'm going to chuck the word diced around a fair bit from now on but the soup can look as neat or as chunky as you wish. In the summer I would replace the beans, cabbage and mushrooms with 2 diced courgettes, 100g/3½oz each of peas and broad beans, 2 peeled, seeded and diced fresh tomatoes and a generous handful of fresh basil and flat leafed parsley.

For 6 people you need:

4 tbsp olive oil
2 medium onions, chopped
3 or 4 cloves garlic, just bruised
1 medium carrot, diced
1 bulb fennel, outer layers removed, diced
1 leek, diced
1 stick celery, diced
1 waxy potato, diced
3 field mushrooms, broken up
dark outer leaves of a small savoy cabbage, or 1 small head of 'cavolo nero'
400g tin of borlotti or canellini beans plus all its juice (or the equivalent weight of home-cooked beans)
400g tin plum tomatoes, squashed and drained of all their juices
1 sprig of rosemary, thyme or 4–5 sage leaves
125g/4oz pasta like ditallini (or macaroni or broken up spaghetti for children), or rice

Heat the oil and gently fry the onions, garlic, carrot, fennel, leek and celery. After about 10 minutes add the potato and cook for 5 minutes. Then add the mushrooms, cabbage, beans and juice, tomatoes and rosemary, thyme or sage.

Simmer for about 20 minutes before loosening with water from a kettle. I'm not going to give exact amounts. You will know how much you need as you do it. By all means use stock and, if you like, add a small amount of meat (bacon is ideal).

When the soup is loose enough you can add the pasta or rice. Your pasta doesn't need to stay al dente (chewy) for minestrone. Neither must the soup be brothy. It really is a meal in a bowl.

Season the soup when it's done, to your own taste. I serve minestrone with either fresh Parmesan or a home-made pesto at the table (or both). I also put out a good extra virgin olive oil. These ingredients allow diners to give their own, final seasoning to the soup.

Mulligatawny. It may be the fare of gentleman's clubs and officers' messes up and down the land, but Mulligatawny has its roots in southern India. 'Milagu Tanni' literally translates as 'pepper water'. It still exists as a wet and fiery version of dhal (lentils) in the state of Tamil Nadu. In the Anglicized version the pulses were discarded. Many versions of mulligatawny contain chicken instead. I always wondered why our colonial forefathers didn't see that the genius of Tamil cookery came from the fact that meat was (and is) anathema to nearly half the local population. There was nothing lacking, nutritionally speaking, about a lentil soup.

Today, you'll find a different version of mulligatawny soup in almost every book that cares to mention it. I'll now throw mine into the ring for good measure. For the truly Anglo-Indian taste you really should use curry powder. Mulligatawny can, like the minestrone on page 47, be vegetarian, or you can include the chicken. Generally, I don't. But at Christmas time it is a good way of using up the last of the turkey. (Yes, you could call it Mulligaturkey). Don't be put off adding the rather surprising, and very un-Indian, grated apple. I can't find any recorded reason for it, but it may have been an attempt to sour the dhal slightly by someone who couldn't get hold of tamarind or kokum (both commonplace in India).

For 6 people you need:

300g/11oz red split peas

3 litres/5¼ pints water or stock

1 stick cinnamon

1 bay leaf

1 onion, peeled and chopped

3 sticks celery, finely chopped

4 cloves garlic, crushed

2 tbsp butter, or ghee (clarified butter available from oriental stores)

1 tbsp Madras curry powder

2 cloves

1 tsp freshly ground black pepper

1 apple, peeled, cored and grated, and tossed in the juice of half a lemon or a whole lime

1 tbsp tomato purée

150g/5oz natural yoghurt

salt

fresh coriander

The following additions are optional:

250g/9oz (or thereabouts) cooked chicken meat

50g/2oz (uncooked weight) basmati or patna rice, boiled and allowed to cool

As a rule, you should only add salt to pulses once they are cooked as it can make them tough. Season this soup at the end of the cooking time.

Boil the split peas vigorously for 10 minutes with half the water or stock. Remove any scum that rises to the surface and, at this stage, keep an eye on things so that the pot does not boil over.

Lower the heat, throw in the cinnamon and bay leaf and continue to cook at a gentle simmer, adding more water or stock as necessary as it thickens. The peas can take anything up to 45 minutes to go soft and fall apart.

In another pan, fry the onions, celery and garlic in the butter or ghee. You can fry them quite hard. Once they are wilting add the curry powder, cloves and pepper. Continue to fry for a couple more minutes, then tip the contents of the pan into the lentil soup.

Add the apple and tomato purée when the lentils are soft and the soup is thickening up. Just before serving add the chicken and/or rice (if using) and check the seasoning. You may want to loosen the soup with more water at this stage. Fold in the yoghurt as you serve the soup. Garnish the mulligatawny with fresh coriander.

Comfort soups. Whilst the tradition of a meal in a bowl offers comfort enough, the following soups have an even more recuperative quality to them, not least because they make great food for those times when we are under the weather. For me all involve the final stage of being whizzed up, and although this is by no means compulsory, there is something incredibly comforting about the velvety texture of a thick, puréed soup. Like mash it can transport us straight back to childhood. Every time I eat a creamed soup I yearn for a bowl decorated with Peter Rabbit skipping around the rim.

The following soups are all about pampering yourself and, as such, they are very 'low maintenance' when it comes to preparation. All of them can be made without stock. Simply follow the method of 'sweating' the main ingredients to leach out their flavours and juices before adding water from a recently boiled kettle. Note that I never use celery when making these soups. This is because I am so lazy that I cannot face the thought of passing soup through a sieve. If you purée a soup made with celery, you must sieve it or face a tangle of stringy bits later. Should the thought of soup without celery make you go pale, simply ignore my attempts to make your life easier and include it.

Potato and watercress soup.

The easiest and in some ways the best. The watercress is almost used like a herb garnish, being added at the end. The variations on this theme are almost limitless. For watercress you could read sorrel, chervil, parsley, chives and so on...

You need:

1 tbsp olive oil (vegetable oil is fine, but olive oil will add flavour)

1 tbsp butter

2 medium onions, chopped

2 cloves garlic, crushed

3 large floury potatoes (Maris Piper are the best), roughly diced

1 tsp salt

1 bunch of watercress, chopped

Gently heat the oil with the butter. Add the onions and garlic and fry them until they are soft and opaque. Do not let them brown. Add the potatoes and salt, stir everything together, turn the heat down really low, and cover. Leave for about 10 minutes; this is your vegetables having their 'sweat'. Check after the 10 minutes are up, and if things are looking a little sticky, add a small amount of recently boiled water from the kettle. Stir and leave again, for another 10 minutes or so. The potatoes should be starting to soften, but do not worry if they are not. Now just cover them with water. They should be only just covered, so around 2 average-sized mugfuls of water (or approx. 400ml/14fl oz) is what you are looking at here. Cook until the potatoes are soft and falling apart. Now the soup can be puréed or even gently broken up with a potato masher in the pot. Be careful if you do this as it can spit like a little volcano as it becomes thicker.

Season the soup to your own taste, and if it seems too thick simply loosen with more hot water. Each time you loosen the soup just check the seasoning.

Add the watercress to the soup in the bowl, or if you like it can be stirred in at the table.

White fish chowder. **For me, the French *soupe de poisson* is the best soup in the world. Sadly, with its shell grinding, flambéing and all round restaurant-ness, it belongs in another book. Here is something very, very easy instead. So easy, in fact, it almost comes as a shock that it turns out so tasty. It isn't a British soup. In fact it comes from Portugal, but the recipe caught my eye some years ago because it seemed odd that it was made with skate. In fact, you can use any white fish, including smoked fish. Skate will give you an extra 'velvety' texture.**

You need:

1 or 2 skate wings (approx 1kg/2lb 4oz)

1 carrot, chopped

1 stick of celery, chopped

1 leek, trimmed and chopped

3 onions, peeled and chopped

4 tbsp extra virgin olive oil

4 cloves garlic, chopped

3 bay leaves

2 large, floury potatoes, peeled and diced

salt, freshly ground black pepper and, if possible, smoked paprika

First, create the stock by cooking the skate. Bring 2 litres/3½ pints of water to simmering point and add the chopped carrot, celery, leek and one of the onions. Let this cook for about 10 minutes, then lower in the skate wings. Do not let the stock boil. Fifteen minutes later, remove the fish with a slotted spoon or fish slice and allow it to cool. It may break up a little as you lift it out but don't worry. Let the rest of the stock carry on cooking.

Pull the flesh of the skate from the bone (which is really just cartilage). It's easy – just run the side of a fork down the wing, starting at the thick end. The meat will come away. Return the bones to the stock.

Now heat about 4 tablespoons of the olive oil in another pan, deep enough for soup. Gently fry the remaining onions, garlic and bay leaves for about 10 minutes. Do not let them brown. Add the potatoes and 1 level tablespoon of salt. Stir everything a couple of times then really lower the heat. Cover the pan and allow the vegetables to sweat for another 10 minutes. If the potatoes are sticking, add one ladleful of the stock (just the liquid though), stir thoroughly and cover again.

Add the fish to the vegetables and stir thoroughly. Now strain the stock and add just enough of it to cover the potatoes in the soup pot. Keep simmering gently until the potatoes are really tender. As soon as they are, lightly mash the soup. Thin it to the texture you like with more stock. Now season it to taste with a little salt. If you can get your hands on the smoked paprika (a Spanish deli is your best bet), garnish the soup with a pinch before serving. That and a generous slug of extra virgin olive oil.

Croutons. **Real croutons are fried. It was once a way to keep stale bread edible for longer. Now that croutons are a luxury rather than an aid to thriftiness, we tend to produce them for soup, and only when entertaining. I bake mine. I leave them pretty rough too. If you want neat cubes, you go ahead.**

Either way, it is best to remove the crusts. I pretty much tear up the bread, lay it on a roasting tray and drizzle it very generously with olive oil. I season it by scattering salt over the entire tray and bake it in a fairly hot oven (180°C/350°F/mark 4) for about 20 minutes. To keep the croutons crispy, never move them from the tray until they are totally cold. If you put warm croutons in a box or bowl they will steam each other and go soft again.

Garlic bread. **Garlic bread is easy, and goes so well with any of the soups in this chapter. When you're making garlic the focus of a recipe though, be careful not to overdo it.**

Really, for a normal sized French stick, you only need 100g/3½ oz of butter and 4 cloves of garlic. I like to infuse the butter and garlic for a fair while. This gives you a less harsh kick from the garlic, as well as intensifying its flavour. Heat your butter on a very low flame and chop the garlic finely. Add the garlic to the hot butter and leave it in a warm place (your hob will be fine, especially if the oven is on) for at least 1 hour. Once the butter is ready, cut into the French stick at intervals of about 2cm/1in, stopping shy of actually slicing it up. Lay it on a large piece of tin foil. Use a spoon or pastry brush to dab a little of the butter onto each 'section' of the bread. If there is butter left pour the rest of it over the stick. Wrap it up in the foil and bake at around 200°C/400°F/mark 6 for 10 minutes before serving.

Cream of spinach soup.

You can use frozen spinach to make this soup. It should be thawed before you start. Weigh out the handy little nuggets.

For 6 people you need:

1 tbsp butter

2 tbsp olive oil

2 medium onions, chopped

1 leek, chopped

2 cloves garlic, chopped

1 floury potato, peeled and diced

2 medium carrots, peeled and chopped

½ nutmeg, grated

500g/1lb 2oz spinach, stalks removed

100ml/3½fl oz milk

salt and pepper to taste

Heat the butter and oil in a pan. Add the onions, leek and garlic and sweat gently until they are soft. Do not let them brown. Add the potatoes, carrots, nutmeg and a generous pinch of salt. Cover and allow to sweat very gently for 10 minutes before adding just enough water to cover the ingredients. Cover again and simmer for about 30 minutes, by which time the vegetables should be very soft.

Add the spinach to the pan and remove from the heat. Stir the spinach into the mixture and leave it to stand for another 10 minutes. The spinach will wilt in the heat of the juices, but should retain its colour. If it looks like it has not cooked down enough after that time just return the pot to a gentle heat for about 5 minutes.

The soup is now ready to purée. Loosen it with the milk. If it seems too thick you can add more milk or water, depending on how luxurious you want it to be. Season to taste when you have the desired consistency. This soup is delicious with grated cheese thrown over the top. Parmesan is the best but a blue cheese works wonders as well.

Cream of tomato soup.

I associate this soup with childhood more than any other. In the days before we all had basil growing in the window this was the last word in tomato soup. I ought to point out that, obviously, it's about as Mediterranean as ketchup. Please don't add any herbs if you want the real, subtle taste to come through.

For 6 people you need:

3 tbsp olive oil

2 medium onions, chopped

2 cloves garlic (optional), chopped or bruised

1 leek, trimmed and chopped

2 large carrots, chopped

1 level tbsp salt

2 medium tins plum tomatoes (total weight 800g/1lb 12oz)

1 tbsp sugar

600ml/1 pint water or stock

300ml/½ pint whole milk

Heat the oil gently in a large pan and add the onions, garlic, leek, carrots and salt. Stir a couple of times, then turn the heat down low. Cover and leave everything to sweat for a good 10 minutes. If your heat is nice and low it will not catch. Keep an eye on it.

Stir the tomatoes and sugar into the vegetables. Bring the heat up high and cook for about 5 minutes, stirring constantly, then add the water or stock. Bring the soup up to simmering point and cook, uncovered, for about 1 hour. All the vegetables should be very tender by this time, but if they are not give it another 15 minutes or so.

Blend the soup and check the flavour. It may need more salt but please avoid pepper. Once the soup has been puréed loosen it with the milk.

Cream of mushroom soup.

Like the tomato soup on page 42, please try this without adding herbs or pepper. It should just taste of mushroom. Be warned, this soup will not be the prettiest to look at.

For 6 people you need:

50g/2oz butter

1 tbsp olive oil

2 medium onions, chopped

2 cloves garlic, chopped or bruised (optional)

2 leeks, trimmed and chopped

1 smallish potato (floury type), diced

1 level tbsp salt

800g/1lb 12oz field mushrooms, washed and chopped (don't skin them for a soup, it's madness)

1 tsp tomato purée

2 tbsp sherry (optional)

1 litre/1¾ pints water or stock

lemon wedges and chopped parsey to garnish (optional)

100ml/3½fl oz double cream, or crème fraîche (optional)

Heat the butter and oil gently in a large pan. Add the onions, garlic, leek, potato and salt and stir. Turn the heat very low, cover and let everything sweat for about 10 minutes. If the heat is low enough the vegetables won't catch, but keep your eye on them.
Throw in the mushrooms and raise the heat. Add the tomato purée, the sherry and about a quarter of the water or stock. Cover and allow to sweat, on high heat, for about 5 minutes.

Add the rest of the water or stock and bring to a simmer. Lower the heat and cook, uncovered, for a further 40 minutes or so.

Blend the soup until it is smooth. (You can serve this soup without puréeing it, which makes it pretty hearty. If you do that, serve it with a wedge of lemon and lots of chopped parsley.) Just pop the cream on the table and let people add it themselves. Or dispense with it altogether.

Golden soup.

Again, I will suggest vegetables, but you can vary them as much as you like. I often use pumpkin rather than swede. A whole orange pumpkin is going to give you a lot of soup so look out for some of the smaller varieties. Onion squash and butternut squash are my favourites.

For 6 people you need:

1 tbsp butter

1 tbsp olive oil

2 medium onions, chopped

2 cloves garlic, crushed

1 large floury potato, peeled and roughly diced

3 carrots, peeled and roughly diced

1 swede, peeled and roughly diced

1 bay leaf

salt and pepper to taste

Heat the butter and oil gently in a pan. Add the onions and garlic and let them soften. Do not let them brown.

Add the vegetables, bay leaf and salt. Stir thoroughly and turn the heat down very low. Cover the pan and leave to 'sweat' for about 10 minutes. Check on them and if they are starting to catch cover them with about 400ml/14fl oz of recently boiled water from the kettle. Cover and leave again, for another 10 minutes. Keep checking and stirring, roughly every 10 minutes, until the vegetables are all soft and look like they will fall apart. Fish out the bay leaf. Now either break up the soup with a potato masher in the pot or purée it. Loosen with water if it seems thick. Season the soup once you have the desired thickness.

Sweet corn and potato chowder. **You can make this soup with sweet corn from the freezer or a tin (I have to say that using the latter is not very sexy). However, come late August and early September, a good greengrocer will have fresh ears of corn on the cob. They make this soup exceptional. You may or may not know the verb 'to shuck'. This is what you do with the corn. Run a pairing knife down the sides of the cob, shearing (or shucking) off the little yellow pellets as you go. Do it into a deep pan or a bowl in a sink because as you mow down the corn, some of it will ping off in unwanted directions.**

For 6 people you need:

3 tbsp olive oil

2 medium onions, peeled and chopped

3 cloves garlic, chopped

1 red chilli (optional), seeded and chopped

2 large, floury potatoes, peeled and chopped

1 tbsp salt

4 cobs of corn, shucked (see above) or 500g/1lb 2oz sweet corn

1 tsp tomato purée

2 litres/3½ pints water or stock

1 tbsp maize flour, or quick cooking polenta (optional)

Heat the oil in a large pan and fry the onions, garlic and chilli (if using) gently for about 10 minutes. Add the potato and salt. Stir everything once and really lower the heat. Cover and allow the vegetables to sweat for about 10 minutes more. It doesn't matter for this soup if they catch a little. If it bothers you just add a couple of tablespoons of water and cover them again.

Add the sweet corn, tomato purée and about half the water or stock. Bring to a simmer and cook until the potatoes are really tender. At this point mash the soup and add the maize flour or polenta (if using). Cook for a further 3 minutes, then loosen the soup with the remaining water or stock until it is as thick as you want it.

You can make this soup with chicken stock, which is delicious. If you have some chicken knocking around add it to the pot with the corn.

A wonderful garnish for sweet corn soup is fresh coriander.

Another is the Moroccan chilli paste, harissa, which can be bought in tins and tubes. You can make it easily at home (in a very ersatz way) by chopping a couple of red chillies with a clove of garlic and half a teaspoon of ground cumin seeds. Add a little salt and loosen the paste with olive oil. If you want to garnish the soup with harissa I suggest you leave the chilli out of the cooking.

A cup of tea. The dried, fermented leaves of the shrub *Camellia sinensis* constitute the world's most popular drink. It was first cultivated in the Far East and was known in Britain as long ago as the seventeenth century. Samuel Pepys mentions tasting it for the first time in 1660. Back then it was regarded as a purely medicinal beverage. This might be why it is still seen as such a soothing drink today, even though it contains caffeine and acts as a stimulant, much like coffee. By the middle of the nineteenth century the shrubs had been introduced to India and Sri Lanka and that was when the popularity of tea soared in this country.

The ritual of taking tea as a meal and/or a social event may have been invented by the Duchess of Bedford sometime around 1830. First it was the preserve of the aristocracy. Lunch was taken very early and dinner much later. Tea served with bread and cake was a way to stave off hunger pangs at five in the afternoon. It soon became a way of showing off fine porcelain and practising one's etiquette, to boot. By contrast, 'high tea' (sometimes known as 'meat tea' or 'Yorkshire tea') became the main evening meal amongst the poorer classes. It marked the end of a hard day's work and some people today still refer to their evening meal as 'tea'.

Ironically, considering its roots as a labourer's dinner, 'high tea' is something we think of as quite decadent and (to use a word I loathe) 'posh'. It might be something to do with the fact that we now use sandwiches, cakes and pastries as quick fixes, grabbed with a coffee on the way to work or in the middle of a trawl round the shops. Can you remember when stopping to eat was a more leisurely affair whatever you were doing? Cafés and tearooms were once the only alternatives to more costly restaurants. They served all manner of toasted sandwiches, egg dishes and some light meals, but now fast food outlets and self-service coffee bars outnumber the old institutions.

The food in this chapter is meant to evoke something of a time gone by, as most comfort food is wont to do. I would encourage everyone reading this to attempt a high tea some time. It needn't be cutesy sandwiches and dinky little cakes. Try something more robust like Welsh rabbit (see page 35) or beans on toast if you fancy it. Do have a go at making a teatime loaf or scones. They are so easy and (unlike that drier-than-you-hoped piece of cake that you grabbed last week in 'cappuccinos-r-us') they never disappoint.

The perfect cuppa. The fact that a chef's bible like *Larousse Gastronomique* contains written instructions for tea-making is testimony to how seriously some people take this drink. There are tea connoisseurs just as there are wine buffs and tasters.

The golden rule seems to be never to use tap water, thus avoiding any hint of chlorine or lime scale. You should use one teaspoon of loose tea per person and then add one 'for the pot'. Teabags are not even mentioned! Just before you put the tea in the pot it should be rinsed inside with a little boiling water. Then, water straight from the kettle (as it boils) should be poured onto the leaves. Tea should brew for just 5 minutes. Stir it just once before pouring through a strainer. An infuser is recommended to stop your tea from stewing in the pot. Milk should be cold and goes into the cup before the tea. There you have it! Most of us tea plebs are so happy with anything 'hot and wet' that all the above may seem like gobbledygook. That said, I just tried making tea following the instructions to the letter and I am currently enjoying a fantastic cuppa. Have a go.

Teatime loaf cakes. We call the following types of cake tea breads because once upon a time that is what they would have been. Cakes were a by-product of bread making and were usually raised with yeast. The invention of baking powder (and then, of course, self-raising flour) in 1850 meant that baking at home became easier and quicker. Not only was baking powder a less temperamental rising agent than yeast, it produced lighter-tasting results. These new tea breads would become cakes to all intents and purposes – something more dainty and elegant to serve with tea than the old yeasted buns and lardy cakes.

I can't stress to you enough just how easy it is to make a delicious fruity loaf. You do need to be around for one or two hours while they cook, but not one takes more than about 10 minutes to put together. The following three recipes will fill an average-sized (20.5cm/8in) domestic loaf tin. They all freeze very well so if you have two tins and a roomy oven it's worth making them in pairs to save one for when you have less time on your hands.

The first two recipes call for a mix of dried fruit and peel. This mix is really down to personal taste. For me it should include currants and raisins, apricots, a little peel and possibly dried fig, which is glorious in all fruit cakes. I like to buy the luxury fruit mixes that you can find in many shops today and keep them in bulk. They dispense with the need to fiddle around weighing various bits and bobs. This may sound petty, but the oddest little things (or the merest hint of 'faffing') can put you off baking. Luxury fruit mixes also mean that I no longer run out of the one kind of dried fruit that I like the most (for me that's apricots, which I invariably pick at till they're gone). How many times have the bakers amongst you headed for the larder only to find that all there is left is a bag of sultanas old enough for a bus pass?

Traditional tea and fruit loaf.

Although this, the most traditional of fruit loaves, is rich and dark, it contains no more fat than the contents of the egg. Which is why (of course) you spread it thickly with butter!

For a 20.5cm/8in loaf tin you need:

- 250ml/9fl oz cold tea, strained of the leaves
- 250g/9oz mixed, dried fruit and peel
- 100g/3½oz walnut pieces
- butter for greasing
- 250g/9oz self-raising flour
- 125g/4oz muscovado sugar
- 1 large egg

First of all (and apologies to anyone who feels that this is patronizing) don't, whatever you do, contrive cold tea. Boil a kettle, make tea and let it go cold. Traditionally this recipe calls for you to marinate the fruits and nuts with the sugar in the cold tea, overnight. You can cheat if you want to make this on a whim. Simply chuck the fruits (not the walnuts) into the tea while it is still hot and walk away for a couple of hours. Add the walnuts only when the tea is cold.

To make the loaf, preheat an oven to 180°C/350°F/gas 4. Grease the loaf tin.

Beat the flour, sugar and egg into the tea mix. Pour into the tin and bake for 1 hour. Lower the heat to 150°C/300°F/gas 2 after that and give it 30 minutes more.

Do not serve the loaf until it is cold. It also matures very well, like most fruit cakes. Try wrapping it up in clingfilm or foil and leaving it in an airtight container for two days.

Cherry and almond cake.

This is a lighter, blonde fruit loaf that looks cute when you slice it to reveal cross-sections of glacé cherry.

For a 20.5cm/8in loaf tin you need:

- 100g/3½oz soft butter (it can be salted if you like. If using unsalted add ½ tsp salt), plus extra for greasing
- 125g/4oz caster sugar
- 3 large eggs
- 50g/2oz ground almonds
- 125g/4oz self-raising flour
- 100g/3½oz glacé cherries
- 50g/2oz golden raisins or sultanas

Preheat the oven to 150°C/300°F/gas 2. Grease and line the loaf tin.

Beat the butter and sugar together until pale and fluffy, then add the eggs, one by one.

Fold in the almonds and the flour, then the fruit. You can leave the cherries whole.

Pour the mixture into the tin and bake for 1½ hours. Because it is a lighter mixture it can sink in the middle, so don't open the oven door for the first hour. Again, allow the cake to cool completely before turning it out and slicing.

'Bara Brith'.

This is my grandmother's recipe for the Welsh tea loaf. Bara Brith means 'speckled bread'. Some recipes still call for a yeasted dough rather than self-raising flour, so this version is not the traditional one. A keen baker could add the fruit, milk and treacle to a bread dough.

My grandmother makes this with dark brown sugar. I am a sucker for using golden caster sugar (a fairly recent discovery for me) so I use that. If you have dark brown sugar knocking around follow this recipe, but substitute golden syrup for the treacle.

For a 20.5cm/8in loaf tin you need:

butter for greasing
300g/11oz self-raising flour
300g/11oz mixed dried fruit
100g/3½oz golden caster sugar, or soft brown sugar
1 tbsp mixed spice
a pinch (about ¼ tsp) salt
1 large egg
100ml/3½fl oz milk
2 tbsp treacle, or golden syrup

Preheat the oven to 180°C/350°F/gas 4. Grease and line the loaf tin.

Mix the flour, fruit, sugar, spice and salt in a bowl. Make a well in the middle and drop in the egg.

Heat the milk until it is just warm and stir in the treacle or syrup until amalgamated. Note that the treacle might curdle the milk slightly, but this is not a problem.

Pour the milk into the well in the flour and beat with a wooden spoon until you have stiff dough.

Pour the mixture into the tin and bake for about 1½ hours. Let the cake go completely cold before you turn it out and serve it. Like the tea bread on page 59, it matures well if stored in an airtight box or tin for two days.

Apple and pumpkin cake.

(Illustrated) People who are suspicious of pumpkin pie should try this. Seek out a robust type of pumpkin. The large 'ironbark' variety has the best flavour and texture, but are on the large side. If you live anywhere near an African or Caribbean grocer's shop they will probably sell pumpkins in very manageable wedges. If pumpkin-hunting is troublesome use carrots instead.

For a 20.5cm/8in cake tin you need:

250g/8oz butter, plus extra for greasing
250g/8oz caster sugar
4 large eggs
100g/3½oz plain flour
50ml/2fl oz milk
125g/4oz ground almonds
1 medium apple, peeled, cored and sliced
200g/7oz pumpkin, peeled and sliced into similar sized pieces as the apple
1 tbsp cinnamon

Preheat the oven to 180°C/350°F/gas 4. Grease and line the cake tin.

Cream half the butter with half the sugar and add 2 of the eggs, one by one. Fold in the flour and then the milk. Spread this batter evenly into the cake tin as the base. Sprinkle it evenly with the ground almonds, then scatter the apple and pumpkin slices over the top. Keep them fairly central, not touching the side of the tin.

For the topping, melt the remaining butter and allow it to stand for 10 minutes. Whisk in the remaining sugar and eggs and the cinnamon and pour it over the cake mixture. Bake the cake for 1 hour, then check it to see if it is firm to the touch. Allow it to cool completely before turning it out and serving. This is delicious with sour cream or yoghurt.

Carrot cake. **We tend to regard carrot cake as a fairly recent import from America (where it is often called Passion cake). In fact it has been here a long time. There are recipes for using carrots in sweet dishes (to avoid the cost of dried fruit and nuts) in *Mrs Beeton's Book of Household Management.* My grandmother says that carrot cake became more popular here during the War because of sugar rationing. She remembers seeing it served at weddings around that time. The sweetness of the vegetables may have negated the need for sugar back then, but you wouldn't know it from the amount used in modern recipes. This is a very sweet cake. The carrots really lend texture and moistness today, and have nothing to do with being thrifty. Icing a carrot cake with cream cheese adds a much needed sharpness to the whole thing.**

For a 20.5cm/8in cake tin you need:

125g/4oz butter, softened, plus extra for greasing

250g/9oz self-raising flour

2 tsp cinnamon

250g/9oz grated carrot

50g/2oz chopped mixed nuts, dried fruit or desiccated coconut (optional)

125g/4oz soft brown sugar

125g/4oz runny honey

juice of 1 lemon

The cream cheese topping:

25g/1oz very soft butter

50g/2oz cream cheese

125g/4oz icing sugar

juice of 1 lemon

Preheat the oven to 180°C/350°F/gas 4. Grease and line the cake tin.

Sift together the flour and cinnamon, then add the carrot and nuts, dried fruit or coconut (if using).

Beat the butter and sugar together until fluffy, then stir in the honey. Fold this mixture into all the dry ingredients and mix well. Loosen with the lemon juice and turn the mixture into the cake tin.

Bake for 1 hour, then check the cake by inserting a skewer or knife into the centre. If it comes out clean the cake is done. If not, keep checking every 10 minutes as you want the carrot cake to be nice and moist. Allow the cake to cool completely before turning out and topping and serving.

For the topping, beat the butter and cheese together briefly and fold in the sugar, then add the lemon juice. Combine these ingredients thoroughly and either spread the icing onto the cold cake or allow people to spoon some onto a plate with a slice. In some ways I prefer to do it that way.

Parsnip and caraway cake.

This is adapted from a Jane Grigson recipe. Even though it sounds very Olde English it was just a happy accident. She was experimenting with a friend's recipe for carrot cake. The cream cheese icing goes well with this too.

For a 20.5cm/8in cake tin you need:

125g/4oz butter, softened, plus extra for greasing
250g/9oz self-raising flour
¼ tsp salt
1 tsp caraway seeds
250g/9oz grated parsnip
125g/4oz chopped walnuts
125g/4oz caster sugar
2 large eggs
2 tbsp walnut oil

Preheat the oven to 180°C/350°F/gas 4. Grease and line the cake tin.

Sift together the flour and salt and stir in the caraway seeds, parsnip and chopped nuts.

Beat the butter and sugar together until fluffy, then add the eggs, one by one. Fold this mixture into the dry ingredients. Loosen it with the walnut oil and turn into the cake tin. Bake for 1 hour, then check the cake by inserting a skewer or knife into the centre. If it comes out clean the cake is ready. If not return it to the oven, and check it every 10 minutes to ensure a moist cake.

Allow the cake to cool completely before turning it out and serving.

Lemon and poppy seed cake.

This can be served like a traditional tea loaf or converted to a rich, sticky cake by dousing it with lemon syrup.

For a 20.5cm/8in cake tine. You need to make 2 separate mixtures for this cake.

For mix 1:

125g/4oz plain flour
1 tsp baking powder
125g/4oz caster sugar
¼ tsp salt
zest of 1 lemon
25g/1oz poppy seeds

For mix 2:

2 large eggs
2 tbsp milk
a dash of vanilla essence (optional)

You also need, on the side:

125g/4oz melted, unsalted butter

Preheat the oven to 180°C/350°F/gas 4. Grease the cake tin.

Thoroughly combine the ingredients of mix 1, add half the ingredients of mix 2 and beat for 1 minute in a food processor or with a large spoon. Add half the butter and beat again until it is fully incorporated.

Now gradually add the rest of mix 2 and the last of the butter, beating for about 30 seconds between each addition.

Pour into the tin and bake for 1 hour. Don't open the oven door during that time because a change in temperature can cause this cake to sink a little in the middle. After an hour, check the cake by inserting a skewer or small knife into the centre. If it comes out clean the cake is ready. Allow it to cool completely before turning it out of the tin.

To make this a 'drizzle cake' heat 125g/4oz sugar in 100ml/3½fl oz of water and stir gently until it has dissolved. Add the juice of 2 lemons and simmer until the mixture coats the back of a spoon. Prick the cooled cake randomly all over with a fork and drizzle over the syrup. This will also make a lovely summertime dessert if you serve the drizzle cake with fresh raspberries and cream.

Soda bread and scones. I have excluded yeast bakery from this book simply because it is a form of home cooking in a league of its own. I am not saying that it is too tricky or too time consuming. Quite the reverse is true, but to start a chapter on bread making (and all the wonderful things you can do with yeast once you have got to grips with it) is really to start a whole new book. I'm not a baker. I love to cook with bread in much the same way that I like to cook with cheese. I like to buy it, well made, by other people.

One type of bread, widely available in Eire, but not so well known here, is soda bread. I will start this chapter with a recipe for it because it is a wonderful addition to the teatime repertoire. To know soda bread is to know a little about scones and griddle cakes. These were all bi-products of the old tradition of designated 'baking days', when the household range would have been stoked up to the max for a frenzy of bread making. It was all done in one day, no doubt, to save on fuel costs. So instead of just using the oven the hob would have been utilized as well. This is how we ended up with such things as Welsh cakes and Scottish pancakes. Scones were probably the result of sweetening up bits of unused flour and soda for a treat. Their size would have meant that they could be slipped into the oven last. Nowadays, far from being a way of using up scraps of dough, they are the centrepieces of (probably) the most indulgent and luxurious way of 'taking tea' in Britain.

Soda bread.

This is hardly bread at all. It is like a great big version of a scone. Easier to make as well. It lends itself beautifully to being eaten straight from the oven with lots of jam and butter. In fact, it doesn't keep well at all so it's best guzzled in one go (you can freeze it by the way). Aside from afternoon tea, it makes a great addition to a ploughman's-type lunch (see page 36).

Soda bread is traditionally made with buttermilk, but instead of hunting around for that I like to sour milk with a squeeze of lemon. If you get hold of buttermilk follow the exact recipe below with that instead of the milk and lemon juice.

For a good-sized loaf you need:

butter for greasing
300ml/½ pint milk
juice of ½ lemon
500g/1lb 2oz bread flour (white or wholemeal or half and half)
1 heaped tsp bicarbonate of soda
2 tsp salt

Preheat the oven to full whack (i.e. 250°C/475°F/gas 9). Grease a baking tray.
Mix the milk and lemon juice in a jug so that the milk curdles.

Mix all the dry ingredients together thoroughly. Make a well in the centre of the bowl and add the milk. Fold the milk into the flour with a spoon then switch to your hands to knead it into a smooth dough. If it is sticky after a good 10 minutes kneading, add a bit more flour.

To make a traditional-looking soda bread, fashion it into an outsized bun shape. Cut a big 'x' in the centre of the top of the bun, place on the baking tray and bake for about 30 minutes. Let it rest for 20 minutes on a cooling rack, and then it's ready to eat.

Scones. (Illustrated on page 65) The centrepiece of one of England's finest traditions is the cream tea: scones, clotted cream and jam are all you need for such an occasion. I promise that a cream tea will be a stupendous affair if you make your own scones and eat them whilst still warm. Don't make them in advance. I say this because scones really do not keep well. That's why they can be a disappointment when bought in from even the most reputable bakers. There are two compensations for this. The first is that they are a doddle to make. The second is that, if frozen quickly (and that means as soon as they are cooled) they can be used at a later date. You just heat them up from frozen.

There are golden rules for scone making. The principles are similar to pastry. Everything bar the flour should be cold. It is even worth chucking the flour into the fridge for an hour or so before you get going. No joke. Your oven, on the other hand, should be pretty fiercely hot. Preheat it well in advance. These rules will ensure the texture will be perfect. But let's get it out in the open now – scones can misbehave. They might rise on a slant (unless you are going to check your dough with a spirit level!) and they might not rise to the dizzy heights of some of the commercial types (that is usually the result of being a bit heavy-handed with the rolling pin). It hardly matters. They will look home-made. Mainly because, well, they are. And that means that they are going to melt in your mouth.

For about 12 scones you need:

500g/1lb 2oz self-raising flour, plus extra for dusting

2 tsp baking powder

325g/11½oz cold butter (plus ½ tsp salt if unsalted)

25g/1oz caster sugar

300ml/½ pint cold milk

Note that I don't add dried fruit to my scones. I really like them plain for a cream tea. By all means throw in 200g/7oz of sultanas or raisins (or even candied peel) if you like. Add them to the dry ingredients and follow the method below.

Preheat the oven to 200°F/400°F/gas 6. Line a baking tray with parchment.

Thoroughly mix the flour and baking powder together. Then rub in the butter until you have a crumby texture. If you have a food processor use it, but 'pulse' the mixture rather than just letting the machine run.

Fold in the sugar (and the fruit if you want it), then add the milk. You should work it in with a spoon at first, but switch to your hands to knead it, quickly as you can, into a spongy dough. It should be soft, but not sticky. If it is sticky just add a little more flour.

Dust a surface lightly with flour and roll the dough out to a thickness of about 2cm/¾in. Using a scone cutter, cut as many scones as you can from this first rolling. If you want to get more from the leftovers make sure that you knead out all creases that cutting the first scones has left.

Put your scones on the tray and bake for about 12 minutes, then let them rest for 5 minutes before eating them. As an alternative to jam, try scones with lemon curd. Fantastic.

Drop scones **(Scottish pancakes). These are really light and are 'pop in the mouth' affairs. They are a bit like a cross between a pancake and a crumpet (not much like a scone at all)! I love to spread them with runny honey.**

For about 12 Scottish pancakes you need:

150g/5oz self-raising flour

2 tsp caster sugar

¼ tsp salt

1 large egg, beaten

150ml/¼ pint milk

butter for greasing

Sift the flour, sugar and salt together. Beat in the egg, then add the milk, bit by bit. You want a batter that is not runny, but just pourable.

Heat a frying pan over a medium heat and lightly coat it with butter. Pour the batter from a tablespoon to make little pancakes. Don't do them too close together in case they spread out. In fact, it's a good idea to test one on its own to see if the pan is hot enough. If it is, the batter will start to bubble and look porous in less than a minute. As soon as this happens flip it over and give it another minute. Let the pancake rest on a plate for another minute before trying it. You can serve these in small stacks, drizzled with honey for a very indulgent (and slightly American) breakfast.

Welsh cakes. **A distant cousin of the scone and Scotch pancake. A crinkly scone cutter makes them look very cute.**

For about 12 Welsh cakes you need:

500g/1lb 2oz self-raising flour, plus extra for dusting

250g/8oz butter

200g/7oz caster sugar, plus extra for dusting

a pinch of salt

a pinch of ground mixed spice

1 large egg

100g/3½oz currants

Rub the flour and butter together. Mix in the sugar, salt, spice, egg and currants. Knead all the ingredients into a stiff dough and allow to rest for 20 minutes.

Flour a chopping board and roll the dough out to a thickness of about 5mm/¼in. Using a scone or biscuit cutter, cut it into rounds.

Heat a large griddle pan or a heavy-bottomed frying pan and cook the rounds quickly over a medium heat. You are essentially making thick pancakes. They are best left a little soft in the middle and they will finish themselves off as they cool so just worry about the outside. You turn them when the underneath is golden brown. When both sides are done drop them onto a tray liberally dusted with caster sugar.

When all the Welsh cakes are in the tray, sprinkle the tops with more sugar. They can be eaten whilst warm (rest them for at least 5 minutes if you plan to do this). They will keep for up to a week in an airtight container.

Saucer pancakes.

As far as I can gather, the habit of cooking these little (French-style) drop scones in saucers may have come from a college hall 'gyp room'. You find gyp rooms in some boarding schools and universities. The phrase comes from a shortening of 'Gyppo' (a nickname for a kitchen servant). The gyppo's are long gone, of course. The modern-day 'gyp room' is a very basic little kitchen with bread, eggs, milk and butter plus tea-making facilities. The students are left to fend for themselves. I have come across a couple of gyp-room recipes whilst researching this book. The worst was easily the 'scrumped' (stolen) corn on the cob from a farmer's field that was boiled in the kettle. These little pancakes were the best.

If like me, you drink all your tea and coffee from a mug, you may be pleased to know that you don't need a set of saucers to make these. If you have the kind of tray used for baking Yorkshire puddings then that's ideal. Otherwise, it is possible to drop spoonfuls of the mixture, spread well apart, onto a hot baking tray.

To easily feed 4 people you need:

- 50g/2oz softened butter, plus extra for greasing
- 50g/2oz caster sugar, plus extra for dusting
- 2 large eggs, separated
- 50g/2oz self-raising flour
- 150ml/¼ pint warm milk

Preheat the oven to 200°C/400°F/gas 6. Grease 6 to 8 saucers or a baking tray with butter and put in the oven.

Beat the butter and sugar together until pale and fluffy. Add the egg yolks, one by one, then fold in the flour. Beat in the milk. Whisk the egg whites to form soft peaks and fold them into the mixture.

Spoon the mixture onto the hot baking tray or into the saucers. If you have a Yorkshire pudding tray you just divide the mixture between each little compartment.

Bake for 15–20 minutes or until golden. Just keep an eye on things. While the pancakes bake, sprinkle more caster sugar generously over another tray. When the pancakes are done drop them into this tray and let them cool, turning once.

Serve these pancakes with jam – they are traditionally eaten folded over a dollop of the jam like a miniature sandwich.

Simple things from a baking tray... As a lazy baker I love to just fill a baking tray with a handful of good ingredients and let the magic happen without me. Flapjacks must be the best example of this. Porridge (give or take a ton of butter and sugar) without stirring. Hooray!

As easy peasy as the following recipes are, there is something a bit 'village fête' about them that implies hours of effort in the kitchen. So if you are having the uninitiated round to tea and they seem impressed by your having baked, ham it up a bit. Rub flour all over an apron. Look a bit 'ruddy' as if you were kneading pastry all morning. As awful as it is, nothing pleases a lazy cook more than being mistaken for some kind of culinary whirling dervish.

Almond slices.

These are related to Bakewell tart (or pudding as it is traditionally called). My grandmother departed with tradition by using plum jam, not raspberry, underneath the almonds. Anyone who has eaten prunes or plums with almonds will know that they were made for each other. Almond slices will keep very well in an airtight container. My grandmother always had a Tupperware box full of them at any one time, kept in the highest cupboard to prevent thieving.

I gave up on almond essence some years ago when I worked in an Italian kitchen. I find the liqueur Amaretto a far less heavy-handed way of flavouring almond pastes. By all means stick with almond essence, but be stingy with it or you will taste nothing else.

For a 20.5cm/8in baking tray (roughly 12 slices) you need:

- butter for greasing
- approx. 250g/9oz shortcrust pastry
- 3 tbsp plum jam
- 2 large eggs, separated
- 200g/7oz caster sugar
- 200g/7oz ground almonds
- 1 level tbsp Amaretto, or ¼ tsp almond essence
- a handful (about 25g/1oz) flaked almonds

Grease a baking tray. Roll the pastry out to line the base and sides of the baking tray. Prick all over with a fork and allow to chill for 30 minutes.

Preheat the oven to 200°C/400°F/gas 6, and if you have a large, flat roasting tray (bigger than the tray with the pastry in) put it on the top shelf of the oven to get hot.

Roughly spread the jam all over the base of the pastry in the baking tray.

Beat the egg yolks and sugar together until pale and fluffy. Add the ground almonds and the Amaretto or almond essence. Whisk the egg whites to soft peaks and fold them into the mix. Turn out onto the pastry, to cover the jam. Sprinkle the top with the flaked almonds and place the tray on the hot roasting tray. Bake for about 30 minutes, or until the almonds are golden brown.

Allow to cool in the baking tray for 10 minutes before turning the tart out onto a cooling rack. Cut into slices when completely cooled.

Flapjacks. **(Illustrated) I include my grandmother's recipe for flapjacks because as far as I know she was the only person who put cornflakes in them. I never found out why. This recipe will work just as well without them. Let me say that it will also work brilliantly (in a trashy sort of way) if you swap the ratio of flakes to oats.**

For about 12 flapjacks (cut from a smallish baking tray) you need:

125g/4oz butter, plus extra for greasing

1 tbsp golden syrup

125g/4oz porridge oats

50g/2oz cornflakes

125g/4oz golden caster sugar

Preheat the oven to 180°C/350°F/gas 4. Grease the baking tray.

Melt the butter and golden syrup in a small pan, then pour them over all the dry ingredients. Mix thoroughly, tip onto the tray and bake for about 20 minutes. If you like a dark, crispy flapjack, cook for 30–35 minutes.

Cut into fingers in the tray while still warm and leave until cooled.

Bread pudding. **Although the ingredients are the same, this is not to be confused with bread and butter pudding (see page 199). Instead, this is a way of using stale bread to make a dense, sticky treat with a crunchy top. You still find bread pudding in the odd baker's shop. My mother liked to serve it with tea like a cake, but it can be eaten warm as a pudding, in which case it needs custard.**

For a 20.5cm/8in baking tray you need:

8 slices of stale bread, crusts removed

300ml/½ pint milk

200g/7oz mixed dried fruit

grated zest of 1 orange

100g/3½oz soft brown sugar

1 tsp mixed spice

50g/2oz melted butter, plus extra for greasing

2 tbsp caster sugar

Preheat the oven to 180°C/350°F/gas 4. Grease the baking tray

Soak the bread in the milk for about 30 minutes then squeeze out all the excess moisture. The best way to do this is to pop the bread into a sieve or colander and place a couple of heavy pots or bowls on top of it.

Put the soaked bread in a large bowl. Mash the bread with a fork until it looks like a fairly smooth porridge, then add the fruit, orange zest, brown sugar, mixed spice and the butter. Stir together well.

Turn the mixture into the baking tray and sprinkle the top with the caster sugar. Cook for 1½ hours. Allow the pudding to cool in the tray for 5–10 minutes before turning it out. This will stop it sticking.

Bonnie

Biscuits. If there is one thing that we manufacture brilliantly as a nation it is biscuits. In fact part of the demise of tea and cakes might be down to how cheap and tasty commercially produced biscuits are. They also keep well. However, there are bad biscuits out there. The fact that some brands see fit to proclaim that their biscuits are 'all butter' or '100% natural' is proof that skimping on the cost of production means depriving you of the good stuff. Of all forms of home baking biscuits are perhaps the fastest and easiest. Children love making them and it's a good way of getting them into the kitchen for the first time. Even the most impatient young chef can handle waiting for as little as 15 minutes to see the fruits of their labour. Here are some simple biscuit recipes.

Ginger biscuits.

These are very quick. They make a great accompaniment to chocolate or vanilla ice-cream.

For about 12 biscuits you need:

50g/2oz butter
125g/4oz golden syrup
1 large egg yolk, beaten
125g/4oz plain flour
50g/2oz dark brown sugar
1 tsp ground ginger
½ tsp bicarbonate of soda
a pinch of salt

Preheat the oven to 180°C/350°F/gas 4. Line a baking tray with silicone paper.

Gently heat the butter in a pan, then add the golden syrup. When both have dissolved into each other remove from the heat and stir in the egg yolk.

Sift together the flour, sugar, ginger, bicarbonate of soda and the salt. Fold them into the butter and egg mix.

You now have a paste that you can roll into small gobstopper-sized balls. Place them a good 3cm/1¼in apart on the baking tray and bake for 15 minutes. Should they spread into each other a little, gently separate them with the edge of a palette knife whilst still warm. They may not be perfectly round, but will still be sexier than ginger nuts. Cool them on a rack (they will crisp up as they cool).

Melting moments.

(Illustrated) So called because they melt a bit as they cook, these are made with cornflakes. They spread to become a thin, brittle biscuit that melts (a second time) in the mouth.

For about 12 biscuits you need:

125g/4oz butter
75g/3oz caster sugar
50g/2oz self-raising flour
2 handfuls of cornflakes (about 15g/½oz. It really is better to risk the 'handful'!)

Preheat the oven to 180°C/350°F/gas 4. Grease and line a baking tray with silicone paper.

Cream the butter and sugar together, then fold in the flour. Sprinkle the cornflakes over the mixture, crushing them as you sprinkle. Then fold them into the mix. Blob teaspoon-sized pieces of the dough onto a baking tray, at least 3cm/1¼in apart, and bake for 20–30 minutes, or until they have browned a little. They will crisp up as they cool.

Currant biscuits.

The joy of dried fruit in a biscuit is the way it gets slightly caramelised and really chewy. Currants are the best for this by a long way, but the following biscuit recipe is very flexible. For currants you could read raisins or even nuts.

For about 12 biscuits you need:

75g/3oz butter, plus extra for greasing

100g/3½oz self-raising flour, plus extra for dusting

½tsp salt

50g/2oz caster sugar

50g/2oz currants

1 large egg, beaten

Rub the butter, flour and salt together. When you have a good crumbly mixture add the sugar and the dried fruit. Add the beaten egg little by little to form a very stiff dough. You may not need all the egg. Shape the dough into a ball and chill it for 30 minutes.

Preheat the oven to 180°C/350°F/gas 4. Grease and line a baking tray.

Dust a work surface with flour and roll out the biscuit dough until it is as thin as you are comfortable with: 5mm/¼in thick is ideal, but don't go mad worrying about the thickness.

Using a round or crinkly cutter, cut out the biscuits and lay them on the baking tray at least 2cm/¾in apart and prick them slightly with a fork.

Bake for 15 minutes, or until pale golden brown. Leave them in the baking tray for about 2 minutes before cooling them on a rack.

Coffee biscuits.

These don't taste of coffee, but are the kind of biscuit that always seemed to come free with coffee when I was younger. They had a vaguely cinnamony, Germanic feel to them. They were also very buttery.

You can make these in a tray, just scored, so that they will break into little rectangles when you want them to. They are very easy to make.

For a 20.5cm/8in baking tray you need:

100g/3½oz butter, plus extra for greasing

100g/3½oz caster sugar

100g/3½oz self-raising flour

¼tsp salt

½ tsp ground cinnamon

Rub all the ingredients together until you have a stiff dough. This is very easy if you have a food processor, but use the pulse button rather than leaving it to run. Allow the finished dough to chill for about 30 minutes.

Preheat the oven to 180°C/350°F/gas 4. Grease and line the baking tray.

Lay out a piece of clingfilm larger than the baking tray. Roll the dough out onto the clingfilm, then invert it so that the biscuit dough falls into the baking tray. Press it in and score with whatever shapes you would like to break it into, then prick each section with a fork. Bake for 20 minutes or until golden, and allow to cool in the tray for 5 minutes before turning out.

Shortbread. 'Short' here refers to crumbliness. Shortbread is literally flour, fat (once they were made with lard) and sugar kneaded into a stiff dough. This can be cut before cooking to make individual biscuits or baked as a flat loaf and broken up later, which is why you sometimes see it sold in wedge shapes. It should be rich and buttery. It should also be 'blonde', and to achieve that you cook it on a low heat for longer than most biscuits. Plain shortbreads cooked this way are more than just tea time biscuits. They can be a good accompaniment for all sorts of light desserts from ice creams to possets and jellies.

Over the years some forms of shortbread have got downright 'fancy' all by themselves. We will come to those shortly (no pun intended).

For about 12 biscuits you need:

125g/4oz butter (salted is best here), plus extra for greasing

50g/2oz caster sugar

175g/6oz plain flour

If making shortbread wedges (see below) preheat the oven to 150°C/300°F/gas 2. Grease and line a baking tray with silicone paper.

Rub all the ingredients together as if you were making pastry or crumble, but keep going until they start to form a very stiff, crumby dough. It does happen so keep going if it all seems too loose. Don't add any liquid!

When the dough forms you have two choices. You can roll it out on a dusted board and cut triangular wedges or you can wrap the dough in clingfilm and roll it into a long, sausage shape. Chill the sausage shape for 1 hour before cutting into thin (5mm/¼in thick) slices for baking. Put the wedges or slices on the baking tray and bake for 1½ hours. Allow the shortbread to cool for 5 minutes or so in the tray before you move them onto a cooling rack to cool completely before eating. Warm shortbread may disappoint as it can be a little sad inside. Like many biscuits, they crisp up as they cool down.

Lemon and semolina shortbread. For semolina you could substitute polenta, which will make the shortbread a very lemony yellow as well.

For about 12 biscuits you need:

100g/3½oz butter

zest and juice of ½ lemon

50g/2oz caster sugar

100g/3½oz plain flour

100g/3½oz semolina flour, or polenta

Rub the butter, lemon zest, sugar and flours, or polenta (if using), together until they start to form a stiff dough. Add the lemon juice and knead the dough into a rough ball. Wrap in clingfilm and roll out into a sausage shape. Chill for 1 hour before cutting out 5mm/¼in thick discs. Preheat the oven to 150°C/300°F/gas 2. Grease a baking tray.

Lay the discs at least 3cm/1¼in apart on the baking tray and cook for 1½ hours. Allow them to cool completely before you eat them.

Millionaire's shortbread.

Thick ingots of this used to lurk around village fêtes and baker's shops when I was a boy. Despite the grand name for this biscuit, old recipes always prescribe cooking chocolate for the topping. Which stingy old millionaire tried to fob his friends off with that awful stuff?

By the way, if you think you have never eaten this, you have probably come across its near relation (I'm trying to avoid saying 'poor cousin') the Twix bar.

I use milk chocolate for this as it seems to go best with the toffee bit. By all means go for dark.

For a 20.5x40.5cm/8x16in baking tray you need:

350–400g/12–14oz shortbread for the base (see page 75)

125g/4oz butter

100g/3½oz caster sugar

2 tbsp golden syrup

200g/7oz condensed milk (this is usually sold in tins of 397g so we are really talking about half a tin. Don't mess up your scales by weighing it out)

200g/7oz milk chocolate, broken up

Preheat the oven to 170°C/325°F/gas 3. Line a baking tray with parchment.

Follow the instructions for shortbread on page 75 (that amount will fit a 20.5cm/8in baking tray) and instead of rolling it into a log press it evenly into the base of the tray. I just use my fingers – as it cooks it tends to level out. Bake the shortbread for 20 minutes then set it aside to cool.

Heat the butter and sugar in a saucepan. When the sugar has dissolved add the syrup and the condensed milk. Bring the mixture to a boil, lower the heat and simmer for 3–4 minutes, stirring constantly. It will thicken and go a toffee colour. As soon as this happens spread it over the shortbread and allow it to cool.

Now melt the chocolate with 4 tablespoons of water, either over a bain marie or in a microwave. As soon as you can, pour it over the toffee and biscuit and even it out with a knife. The reason I add a little water to the chocolate is so that I can effortlessly pour it on, and not have to even it out. You get a glossy smooth topping and it doesn't set totally brittle, so it is easier to eat later. Talking of later, you must chill the shortbread for at least 1 hour to let it set. Cut it into whatever kind of slices you like, it cuts easily. Once it is made it can be kept in the fridge for about a week, if it lasts that long.

A night in

A sack of potatoes. Once a foreign interloper in the kitchens of northern Europe, the potato has become our staple. It is the cornerstone of 'meat and two veg' (a cliché that, for some, defines British cooking). Whether roasted, baked, mashed or chipped, we love to dig into potatoes. Strangely, we are not the connoisseurs we should be when it comes to the tuber we claim to revere. There are endless, excellent varieties of potato in existence. Enthusiasts wait eagerly for the first Jersey Royals of spring and the Pink Fir Apples of autumn, but few of us really know one type of potato from another.

Part of the problem is the way that potatoes are sold. Recently I checked out my local supermarket and found myself gazing at yard upon yard of washed, neatly bagged, generic-looking spuds, complete with cooking instructions. As a lazy cook it saddens me to acknowledge that storing washed potatoes does nothing for their flavour or their shelf life, but this is a fact. There is a reason for those old-fashioned, heavy white bags full of grubby potatoes down at the greengrocers. Potatoes do not like bright supermarket lights any more than they want to be imprisoned in polythene. Over exposure to light causes them to go green and bitter. Buy loose, unwashed potatoes and store them in a cool dark place, preferably not the fridge.

I keep a sorry looking old nailbrush by the kitchen sink for the express purpose of scrubbing potatoes. The short burst of labour involved is a small price to pay for flavour.

Cooking instructions for the potatoes that you find on supermarket shelves are very helpful indeed, but once you get to know your potato varieties (they will be printed on the packaging) you can start to make your own choices about which types work best for you. What's more you will have joined an elite section of society, the type of person who might grow their own or who simply nods sagely when listening to afternoon shows on Radio 4.

A simple plate of boiled potatoes. **New potatoes are unbeatable when it comes to this, the simplest of treatments. The best and more seasonal varieties available in Britain are Jersey Royals: tiny and expensive, but worth it. They appear in early spring and many consider them to be the last word in new potatoes. They are waxy, slightly sweet and earthy tasting. Soon after the first flush of the Royals come the Mids, slightly larger, but still bursting with flavour. The Jersey Ware, later and larger still, marks the end of the season. One oddly named new crop potato appears in autumn. The Pink Fir Apple is as knobbly and ill-shaped as a piece of ginger, yellow-fleshed, waxy and creamy all at once; it is my favourite new potato.**

We tend to associate new potatoes with summer, but the French Ratte (a.k.a. Belle de Fontaine) is the best of those available year round. It is slightly knobbly and cylindrical with a waxy yellow flesh. Avoid the suspiciously nameless 'washed mids' you see everywhere. Another good, year-round new potato is the red-skinned, small Roseval. It is very waxy, but is an acquired taste as it has a sharp, lemony flavour.

I always start cooking boiled potatoes using cold, slightly salted water. Some people prescribe throwing new potatoes into rapidly boiling water to improve flavour and texture, but the risk of over-filling the pan and dousing the hob (or worse still your hand) puts me off. Cold potatoes also draw the heat out of the hot water so that there is little point to this. Only just cover the potatoes with the water, and once it is boiling reduce it to a gentle simmer, and cover. Test them with a fork or a skewer before draining them thoroughly. Giving cooking times for potatoes is tricky, as it depends largely on how cold they were when you put them in the pan. Everyone seems to have their own idea about how well done they like a new potato to be. I am of the slightly overdone school, since they gobble up more of whatever I am going to douse them in when ready (usually butter and a herb of some description).

The easiest potato salad ever. **I must admit that I am fonder of new potatoes at room temperature than hot. This is because of this 'sort of' salad from my childhood. Next to simple grilled fish or a chop it is summer on a plate, all year round.**

Whilst the new potatoes are boiling, finely chop a shallot, a handful of mint or chervil and a handful of parsley. You can add any other bits and bobs you fancy. Capers are good, radishes are even better. Celery heart is also lovely. Mix the ingredients in a large bowl and sprinkle with sea salt (and pepper if you wish). When I was young this salad was dressed with vinaigrette, but I am now a convert to plain extra virgin olive oil, sea salt and nothing else. As soon as the potatoes are done, drain them well and spread them on a tray. While they are still warm attack them very gently with a fork, bruising them if they are tiny Jerseys or cutting them in half if they are larger. Again, while still warm toss them with the other ingredients. Bits of debris from where you attacked your potatoes will cause ever such a slight emulsification of the dressing, which is the joy of this salad.

Roasting, chipping, baking and mashing. This is where a potato buff comes into his or her own, because the type of flesh that a potato has is crucial to how it should be treated. You need to know your waxy from your floury. Waxy potatoes tend to be yellow-fleshed and take longer to break up during cooking. Floury potatoes are paler-fleshed and go fluffy and soggy fairly swiftly. If that sounds like a culinary disaster fear not: sometimes this is exactly what you want. The best way to explain all the above is to point out which variety works best with each cooking method. Read the following section and impress the hell out of your greengrocer next time you are potato shopping.

Roasting. Few things rob people of life's real pleasures more than instant (frozen) roast potatoes. They smell and taste of scary, Seaside Hotel lunches. They exist merely because so many people claim to be bad at making their own. Successful potato roasting, which is actually a cinch, brings with it a disproportionate sense of achievement. This is as good a reason as any for having a go.

Two recipes for roasting potatoes follow: one is the classic Sunday Lunch type, the other is a glorified 'oven chip'. Both are very low maintenance, but the chippy kind is possibly the easiest.

Classic roast potatoes. Floury potatoes are essential. Maris Piper and Mature King Edwards are superb because they start to disintegrate quickly when boiled. How many you need depends on the size of the potatoes and how hungry you are. I find a medium-sized potato (about 200g/7oz if you want to go by weight) per person yields more than enough. You want to peel, then cut them into rough quarters, and bring them to a rapid boil in plenty of salted water. Check after about 5 minutes. What you are looking for is not a cooked potato, but one that has gone a little fluffy around the edges. The fluffy part will give the potato a crispy shell. Drain the potatoes thoroughly in a colander and leave to one side.

The flavour of the potatoes depends largely on the fat that you roast them in. There is a widely accepted wisdom that duck or goose fat is second to none. However, if you are a Sunday-roast kind of person then hopefully you have saved some dripping or lard from last week's joint. Be aware that lamb dripping has a very distinctive 'lamby' taste. Vegetable oil is okay, but olive oil can overpower the sweetness of good potatoes. Butter will give a nutty, slightly caramelized flavour.

The hotter the oven, the better the roasty. Full whack (by which I mean around 250°C/475°F/gas 9). If you are serving the potatoes next to a roasted joint of meat or poultry you want to get them into the oven about 40 minutes before serving. Use a heavy-bottomed roasting tin. Heat the fat (a generous tablespoon will do enough potatoes for 4 people) on the hob before carefully adding the spuds. Adding the potatoes before the fat is hot enough is what makes them stick to the tray. To make sure the fat is hot enough you can add just one as a tester. It should fizz healthily as it touches the fat. Carefully shake the potatoes and make sure they are all coated with the fat. Season very lightly with salt and place them in the oven. About halfway through the cooking time you can turn the potatoes if you wish. I never do, I simply rebaste them with the surrounding fat.

Oven chips. **The second type of roasting goes well with lighter dishes such as fish or chops, and I call these kind of roast potatoes 'posh oven chips'. Waxy-fleshed potatoes are perfect for this method. Look for the large new crop Jersey Ware or the imported Spunta and Cyprus varieties.**

For 4 people you need about 6 large new potatoes (or about 200g/7oz per person if you prefer to go by weight) and 3 tablespoons of butter or olive oil. You can peel the potatoes but they are great with the skins left on. There is no need for pre-boiling and this method takes about 1 hour with the oven at 200°–220°C/400°–425°F/gas 6–7. Preheat a roasting tray with the butter or oil for about 5 minutes. Cut the potatoes into quarter-sized wedges and add them straight to the hot fat in the roasting tray. Season with a little salt before putting them in the oven.

Adding a chopped sprig of rosemary, sage or thyme halfway through the cooking time adds character to these potatoes. They are delicious with mayonnaise.

Chips. **I have to admit that, for me, the comfort involved in eating chips is largely derived from tearing open the paper they were wrapped in, whilst relishing the thought of not having to wash up. To deep-fry your own chips is, frankly, a bit of a palaver. Unless you have a deep-fat fryer you need a wide, heavy-bottomed saucepan and a chip basket for starters. Not to mention a crinkle cutter (I made that last bit up). However, should you be reading this a long way from a fish and chip shop and have not discovered crinkle cut oven chips (poor thing, where are you?) here goes...**

Use King Edwards or Maris Pipers: good, floury types. Peel and slice them thickly before cutting into chips. Then wash and dry them thoroughly to remove excess starch. Wet spuds and hot fat are a scary combination. Line a baking tray or large plate with kitchen towel and put to one side.

Fill the saucepan no more than one-third full with either lard, dripping or groundnut oil (the best vegetarian option). Heat it to about 190°C/375°F. A deep-fat fryer or a temperature probe (a thermometer will crack) takes the guesswork out of this. Otherwise, the best way to tell is to put one chip in and if it bubbles healthily and starts to brown a little in less than 1 minute, the rest can follow. Turn the heat down to medium and fry them all for no more than 5 minutes. The heat will have lowered at this point and they will not brown, but good chips are always twice cooked. Take them out of the oil and rest them for 2 minutes while you bring the temperature of the fat back up to about 200°C/400°F on a high flame. Please don't wander off anywhere (it just takes 2 minutes to get that way). Pop the chips back in. They should take about 3 minutes more to go golden and crispy. Again, don't go anywhere. Watch them like a hawk. When they are ready remove them from the fat and give them a very gentle shiver whilst still over the pan. Turn off the stove. Then transfer the chips to the kitchen towel to remove excess fat. Eat immediately.

(Cheating at) **Bubble and squeak.** **Traditionally, bubble and squeak is made by frying up leftover potatoes and cabbage (or Brussels sprouts at Christmas) with dripping from a roast joint of meat. Some say this dish is named by the noise of the frying vegetables, but there is also a theory that suggests it has something to do with the effect of brassica on the digestive system. Let's not dwell on it. Such subject matter hardly whets the appetite. Since sprouts are so seasonal (and since most people are so squeamish about them), I have a cheat's version of this dish, which can be made 'today-rather-than-tomorrow'. You can use just about any green cabbage. Savoy works best for me. The quantity of cabbage in a bubble and squeak is really down to you. If you like it more starchy than 'cabbagey' just use less. Lately I have replaced the dripping with a knob of butter, as it adds a slightly caramel note to the whole thing.**

For 4 people you need:

3 medium waxy-fleshed potatoes, roughly diced into 2cm/¾in(ish) cubes

2 tbsp butter, lard or dripping

a splash of olive oil

2 medium onions, peeled and roughly chopped

approx. ½ Savoy cabbage (or similar), cored and roughly chopped

Optional extras:

150g/5oz diced smoked bacon

about 6 or 7 sage leaves

1 or 2 cloves garlic, chopped

3 or 4 juniper berries, crushed

There are two ways to make this version of bubble and squeak. One is to slam it in the oven in a roasting tray, and the other is to fry it all the way in a pan. I love the roasted version because the cabbage gets slightly crispy on the top and reminds me of that phoney Chinese seaweed dish (really fried kale but who's complaining)!

Boil the potatoes in salted water until they are just tender. They will probably take about 15 minutes, but check them after 10 and again before draining. As soon as the potatoes are done put them to one side.

If you are going to bake this dish, make sure you preheat the oven to about 200°C/400°F/gas 6. Place a large baking dish in the oven to warm.

Heat half the butter or fat in a wide skillet or frying pan. Add the olive oil, which will stop it from burning. Fry the onions, on quite a high heat, so that they start to catch ever so slightly. When they do this throw in the bacon, if you are using it, plus any herbs, garlic or spices. Give them about 5 minutes in the pan, stirring regularly. Add the chopped cabbage and stir-fry it with the other ingredients until it wilts. This could take about 5 minutes or so. Transfer the potatoes to a mixing bowl and add the fried ingredients. Season with a pinch of salt.

Remove the baking tray from the oven and put the remaining butter or fat into it. When it has melted add the other ingredients and return to the oven for about 20 minutes, or until the bubble and squeak has browned.

There are few things that go better with this dish than fried eggs, with the yolks still soft.

Jacket potatoes. Some things in life were never meant to happen quickly. A baked potato is one of them. King Edwards or Desiree, at about 400g/14oz each in weight (i.e. on the large side) are the best for eating in the jacket. You can stick a skewer through the potato or blast it in a microwave and finish it in the oven, but you will only compromise the experience. A good baked potato needs to be scrubbed clean, scored with an x on one side, sprinkled with sea salt and baked for 1½ hours until it is molten and fluffy in the middle with a crispy skin. In fact if you have a modern, fan-assisted oven a 400g/14oz King Edward can take as little as 55 minutes. Trust me; I'm looking at one as I write this. It goes into the oven at 190°C/375°F/gas 5 and demands no more of your attention than a quick test with a fork or skewer to see that it is soft all the way through. It doesn't get any easier. Nothing beats the comfort given by mashing the flesh of a jacket potato with an obscene amount of butter, but some alternatives follow.

A few easy toppings or fillings:

Real tuna mayonnaise. Few things go as well with a jacket potato as tuna mayonnaise. Try this recipe for the real thing given to me by Trish Hilferty of the Fox Dining Room in London. A similar version is served there as the sauce for Vitello Tonnato, a traditional Italian salad with veal or capon.

Note the fact that this is real mayonnaise. If you are pregnant or elderly, or merely worried about raw eggs simply omit them and the olive oil, and use about 250ml/9fl oz of ready-made mayonnaise (not salad cream) instead. Hellmann's is the obvious choice; nothing else beats it for flavour.

For 4 people you need:

2 free-range, organic egg yolks (please don't consider using anything else, especially for eating raw)

2 tsp Dijon mustard

1 gherkin, chopped, plus 1 tbsp of vinegar from the jar

300ml/½ pint olive oil (avoid extra virgin for this as the taste is too strong)

125g/4oz good-quality tinned tuna in oil, drained and mashed lightly

4 anchovy fillets

1 tsp capers, washed and squeezed to remove excess moisture, then chopped

salt and pepper to taste

Using a food processor or a whisk, beat the eggs with the mustard and the vinegar from the gherkin jar.

Add the oil, slowly at first, but faster as it begins to thicken and emulsify. Remove to a mixing bowl and add the gherkin, tuna, anchovies and capers. Taste and season as neccessary – bear in mind you are using anchovies and capers, both salty. Keep this in the fridge until you are ready to serve it.

Other additions can be included if you like. A chopped red onion or a couple of tomatoes are ideal.

Watercress, red onions and soured cream. **If you don't fancy indulging in soured cream you can use crème fraîche, cottage cheese or Greek yoghurt, as they tend to have a lower fat content.**

For 4 people you need:

- ½ small cucumber, peeled
- 1 red onion, peeled and finely chopped
- 1 bag (or bunch) of watercress, roughly chopped
- 1 tbsp olive oil
- 150ml/¼ pint soured cream
- juice of ½ lemon
- salt and pepper to taste

Cut the cucumber in half along its length and run a teaspoon gently down the seed cavity to remove them. You don't have to do this, but it reduces the water content of the cucumber. Now chop the flesh into fine dice like the onion.

Combine the cucumber, onion and watercress with the oil, then stir in the soured cream. Finally season with the lemon juice, salt and pepper before serving over the potatoes.

Spam stuffing. **I say Spam but really any cooked ham or bacon will do. Spam is an excellent standby if you have it around and children seem to love it. Stuffed jacket potatoes make excellent children's food and, should there be a period when they are being anti-vegetable in general, the skin is a good source of fibre. Green veg can actually be chopped into the filling or used instead of the ham; garden peas or broccoli are good.**

For 4 people you need:

- 4 baking potatoes
- 350g/12oz chopped Spam
- 2 tbsp butter
- approx. 125g/4oz grated Cheddar cheese

Cook the potatoes thoroughly in their jackets (see page 86) and, when ready, cut them in half down the length before leaving to cool for about 10 minutes. Leave the oven on.

When there is less danger of burning your hands, scoop all the flesh out of the potatoes and combine it with the chopped meat and butter. Mash it back into the potatoes and top with the grated cheese. Return to the oven for another 10 minutes or so, until the cheese has grilled nicely and turned golden brown.

Rabbits in jackets. **Ghastly name. I instantly think of the hapless Peter, lost in Mr McGregor's garden.**

Never fear, this meal is guiltlessly vegetarian. It is great for fireworks night. Double the quantity for Welsh rabbit (see page 35) and bake 4 large potatoes (see opposite). When they are done, cut each in half down the length and, when cool enough to handle, scoop out the inside flesh. Mash the potato flesh into the rabbit mix and return to the jackets. Grill until browned on top.

Mash. **Mashed potatoes enjoy pride of place in this book, because for many of us they make essential comfort eating. But you do not want to cook such a beloved national treasure with the wrong potato. Waxy types make gluey mash. They simply do not break down enough to produce the right texture. Maris Piper, Marfona and Estima make excellent mash. How many potatoes you use depends on how big they are and on the appetites of those about to eat them. I tend to go on 1–1½ medium-sized potatoes per person.**

The potatoes need to be cooked in a pan large enough to do the mashing in afterwards. High-sided, narrower pans are the best. It is also worthwhile giving yourself enough time to cook the potatoes whole, as this definitely improves flavour. Just cover them with salted water, bring them to the boil then simmer with a tight-fitting lid until they are very, very tender. Impatient mash makers get lumps. Any number of cookbook writers have extolled the use of hand-held whisks or of squishing potatoes through sieves. I only ever use a masher. Drain the potatoes thoroughly. Whilst they are draining return the pan to the heat with the milk and butter for the mash. Let them heat through. Quantities of milk, cream and butter vary according to taste, but I tend to use about 100ml/3½fl oz of milk (or cream, or half and half of each) and a very generous tablespoon of butter (approx 50g/2oz) for 4 people. Return the potatoes to the pan and mash, off the heat, until there are no lumps. At this stage it is worth whipping them with a wooden spoon for about 30 seconds to fluff up the whole shebang. Season to taste with salt. I tend to leave pepper out of mash in case it features in whatever goes with it.

Eating mash. Mash is best eaten as soon as it is cooked. The nature of the starches in the potatoes changes after a while so that the flavour and texture deteriorates (remember school mash?) when it sits around for too long. It is best not to cook the potatoes far in advance of a mealtime. The very nature of mash means that it should form the centrepiece of very simple meals so this will not present any problems for you.

Variations:

Adding a root vegetable like parsnips or celeriac. Use 2 parsnips or 1 celeriac per potato. They have a higher water content than potatoes and take a little longer to cook, so cut them to about half the size of the potatoes and go easy on the milk when you mash.

Adding horseradish. This is delicious. Ask your local greengrocer to get some fresh horseradish for you. It looks like a long, knobbly parsnip. If doing mash for 4 people you should use about a quarter of a root of grated horseradish. This may seem like a conservative amount, but mash should not be overwhelmed by any one flavour (which is why I tend to omit black pepper from mine). Grate the horseradish with the blade you would use for Cheddar cheese. The root can be extremely fibrous, worse than ginger. Oh, and stand outside... or at least near an open window. There will be tears if you don't! Add the grated horseradish to the butter and milk when you heat them. The milk may look like it has curdled slightly. Do not be put off by this, as all will come good when you mash the potatoes. Horseradish mash and poached salmon is wonderful.

Adding nutmeg. Grate a very conservative amount (a quarter of a nutmeg is plenty for 4 people) into the finished mash. Nutmeg mash is wonderful with beef casserole.

Adding garlic. For garlic mash to taste good it is essential that the garlic is cooked first. Raw garlic will overwhelm the other ingredients, as will too much garlic. One clove per person is a good rule of thumb. Roast a whole bulb wrapped in foil, for about 30 minutes at 190°C/37°F/gas 5. Allow the garlic to cool, then squeeze the flesh from as many cloves as you fancy into the potatoes when you add the milk and butter. You can keep roast garlic in the fridge to use as a purée or a spread later.

Adding spring onions (Champ). Champ is mashed potatoes the Irish way. You must use yellowy, salted butter. You could be ultra pedantic and use Irish salted butter since it is widely available and generally excellent. If doing mash for 4 people use a bunch of spring onions (that is, at least 6 heads). You want them very fresh so that you can use them from green top to white toe. Sometimes they develop an ever so slightly fibrous outer skin, like leeks, which you can remove by nicking them very slightly with a fruit knife. Remove the little beard at the white end and chop the rest of the onion. Heat the milk and half the butter 20 minutes before the potatoes will be done. Add the spring onions and simmer gently. When the potatoes are done add the rest of the butter to them and mash. When the mash is smooth, fold in the spring onions and milk. Season and loosen with more milk or butter if needs be.

If you can get hold of **salt cod** (smoked haddock will also do), a generous fillet, boned and skinned, can be poached and then flaked into this dish for a heartwarming meal.

Adding leek and cabbage (colcannon). Another Irish version of mash. This time (assuming there are 4 of you again) sauté 2 leeks and the inner leaves of a small savoy cabbage in a tablespoon of butter or oil until tender before folding them into the mash. Season to taste. I love to grill the finished colcannon with a fairly soft Irish cheese called Durrus to make a meal of it. Any good cheese of your own choosing will do just as well. The results are delicious. There is an old custom of serving both champ and colcannon pressed round the sides of a dish with a well for the butter in the middle. No doubt this was a way of giving extra fat content and therefore sustenance to what were once essentially peasant meals. These days of course such habits amount to pure indulgence.

Corned beef hash. **Cooked, salted beef tinned in its own fat and jelly came to Britain from America around the time of the First World War, and was known as bully beef. It is a distant cousin to salted brisket and hash can be made with the fresh stuff if you have a way of getting hold of it (ask a good butcher). It needs to be fully cooked, and then shredded for this dish. Since brisket requires a long slow cooking time most people make hash with the tinned version. Adding peas was a peculiarity of my father's, but since he taught me this dish I will include them in the recipe below. You need not add them if you balk at the idea, but the sweetness of peas cuts through the saltiness of this meal very nicely.**

For 4 people you need:

1 large onion, peeled and chopped

2 tbsp dripping, or oil

500g/1lb 2oz corned beef or cooked salt beef

1 tin chopped plum tomatoes, drained and juice reserved

450g/1lb peas, blanched if fresh, thawed if frozen

3 medium potatoes, cooked and mashed with a little butter

a dash of Worcestershire sauce, or Tabasco (optional)

salt and pepper to taste

Fry the onion in the dripping or oil, quite hard, for about 5 minutes. It is okay if it catches a little. Add the meat, tomatoes and peas to the onion and when it is all simmering away nicely season to your own level of saltiness (go very easy on the salt because of the meat). If the mixture seems dry by all means add the juice from the tomatoes.

Finally, fold the potatoes into the other ingredients and check the seasoning again. This is the point at which you can add the Worcestershire sauce if you like.

I love to grill corned beef hash until the top is golden brown. It makes a great hangover brunch served with poached or fried eggs. Tomato ketchup is also mandatory.

Over mash. The following meals took their shape from the three most popular answers to a sort of questionnaire I bullied all my friends into answering. Assuming that what follows is fare for a comfy night in, I have given quantities relevant for a couple of diners.

Liver and bacon.

Liver, bacon and onions were made for each other, but this would be so low down on some people's list of good things to eat. The reason is invariably an association between this meal and school dinners. What was that all about? Was there a manual in school kitchens up and down the land called 'How to Make Children Hate Liver'? Once it has been overcooked, liver is irredeemable. Not only does it become tough and powdery, it takes on a bitter taste. The best way to get around spoiling the liver is to make this instead of a casserole and it takes less time.

For 2 people you need:

- 2 tbsp plain flour
- a pinch of salt
- a pinch of pepper
- 2 generous, evenly cut slices of liver, about 1.5cm/¾in thick (ask the butcher to do it for you)
- 1 tbsp butter
- 4 slices of smoked bacon or pancetta, cut into strips
- 3 or 4 sage leaves
- 1 medium onion, finely sliced
- 1 glass red wine
- 1 tsp tomato purée
- a tiny pinch of sugar

Have the mash ready before you start the liver. With a tight-fitting lid on the pan you will not lose heat from the mash.

Season the flour with the salt and pepper and sprinkle it over a tray or large plate. Dust the liver slices with the flour and set aside.

Heat a heavy-bottomed pan or skillet and melt half the butter in it. Fry the bacon or pancetta strips until they are as done as you like them (I'm a crispy bacon man, but each to his own). Remove them with a slotted spoon and put to one side. Leave the fat in the pan and fry the sage and onion until nicely wilted. They should only take a couple of minutes on a high heat. If the onion catches a little, so much the better. Remove from the pan and put to one side.

Now fry the liver. For pink liver you need to give it about 2 minutes on each side over a fairly high heat. When it is done, lift it out and plonk straight on top of the mash. The last bit is incredibly quick and easy.

Let the pan get hot again and immediately throw in the onion and the bacon. Pour in the red wine and let the whole thing bubble up. Sometimes, if the red wine is very boozy, you will get a little flambé action. It doesn't always happen and it needn't. If the alcohol doesn't burn off it will evaporate anyway. Should you, bizarrely, be seducing someone with liver and bacon you may want to be sure of the flames, in which case fortify the wine with a very small slug of brandy.

Once the wine has bubbled up, quickly season it with the tomato purée, the remaining butter, salt, pepper and, if you like, the sugar (if the wine was quite a fruity one you might want to omit it). Douse the liver in your new gravy and tuck in.

Onion gravy for sausages.

Onion gravy is so easy to make, but it can be dull if you are not patient. Coaxing tender, silky sweetness from the onions just doesn't happen all that fast. Make it before everything else. Let's face it, if you are having it with sausages and mash the only other chore you face is grilling the sausages and boiling some spuds.

For enough to feed 4 people you need:

1 tbsp butter

1 tbsp olive oil

3 red onions (for they are sexiest), peeled, halved, then sliced

1 clove garlic (optional)

3 or 4 sage leaves

a handy bottle Masala or Madeira wine, or red wine plus 1 level tsp sugar

1 tsp Dijon or wholegrain mustard

salt and pepper to taste

Heat the butter and oil in a heavy-bottomed frying pan. When hot, add the onions and begin to fry gently. You don't want them to catch, but don't go mad if they do. Some people like that.

After about 5 minutes add the chopped sage and the garlic (if using).

After about 20 minutes on a gentle heat, and really not before, add about 300ml/½ pint of the wine and whack up the heat so that everything is really bubbling. If you are using plonk, just add the sugar to bully a sweet dimension out of it. You need not if you don't care for it. After about 2 minutes of bubbling, sniff the pan. The alcohol should have evaporated and you'll know it has not if you get a pungent smell. If you do, cook for another minute before turning down the heat. Turn the heat down when happy and boil a kettle of water. Stir the mustard into the pan and cook for a final 5 minutes. If it all looks a little too dry at this point (and by that I mean dryer than what you want all over your mash) add a splash of water from the kettle. Season with salt and perhaps pepper at the end of the cooking.

You can make this as far in advance of your meal as you like and of course it is fine to make a large quantity and freeze some.

'Chilli' sauce.

There is no chilli in this sweet relish, just red pepper. You could give it some heat if you like, but it is charming just as it is. Try it with sausages. My family eats it with shepherd's pie. Try it! The recipe is very quick and easy. You could follow the quantities below to make a bowlful for the table or multiply it to make a few jars. It keeps very well.

You will need:

6 tomatoes, peeled and finely chopped

1 small onion, finely chopped

1 sweet red pepper, finely chopped

100ml/3½fl oz wine vinegar

100g/3½oz caster sugar

1 level tsp salt

Heat the vegetables with all the other ingredients and simmer until the mixture has thickened and reduced by about a third. This will take about 30 minutes. Allow to cool completely for the sauce to set. If you are keeping this in a jar it is best stored in the fridge.

Braised cod and parsley sauce (in one pan).

I say cod, since that and parsley sauce is the famous combination. Any white fish will work here. It's important to buy fish in a responsible way. For me, that means talking to those in the know. Ask a local fishmonger what you should be buying, and how it was caught. Line-caught fish has the least impact on the environment. Boycotting this and that because of the latest hysterical headline is not going to help the fish or fishermen.

Be warned, this meal will not rock your world unless you hanker for the soft and fairly bland fishiness that it imparts. It is real old-fashioned nursery stuff, but it beats the 'boil in the bag' version for me.

For 2 people you need:

2 tsp soft butter
1 tbsp olive oil
2 x 250–300g/9–11oz fillets of white fish, skin on
¼ onion
450ml/¾pint milk
1 bay leaf
1 heaped tsp plain flour
a generous handful of curly or flat leaf parsley, roughly chopped
some hot fish stock, or a kettleful of boiled water
salt and pepper to taste

Have your mash ready.

Heat 1 teaspoon of the butter and all the oil in a heavy-bottomed frying pan wide enough for the two fillets of fish. Seek out a lid from one of your saucepans that will cover the frying pan. When the pan is hot enough and the butter fizzing nicely, place the fish in, skin side up. Chuck in the onion and fry for about 2 minutes. Give the pan a little shake at this point to check that the fish has not stuck. Do not worry unduly if it has, just nudge it with a palette knife or fish slice.

Add the milk and bring up the level of liquid to just cover the fish with the fish stock or water from the kettle. Add the bay leaf with a pinch of salt and pepper. Simmer, covered, for about 7 minutes or until the fish is cooked through. This really will depend on the thickness of the fillet. Cooked cod will yield easily to a gentle touch. It feels like a soft cushion. Immediately lift the fish out of the pan and place it on the mash, on a warmed plate. The last part is quick.

Discard the bay leaf, then pour the remaining liquid from the pan into a bowl or jug and set aside. Fish out the onion if you wish, or break it up with the end of the spoon if you don't. Add the second teaspoon of butter to the pan and heat it quickly. As soon as it is fizzing, add the flour and stir in with a wooden spoon. It looks lumpy; it's okay, this is the beginnings of the sauce. Add the liquid from the fish, bit by bit, until it has incorporated all the flour and butter, then stir and thicken until it coats the back of a spoon. If it seems to be too thick (and this will depend on whether you lost much fish liquor whilst simmering) just add more water or stock. Finally, season and add the parsley, just folding it into the sauce before pouring it over the cod.

Eat immediately.

Potato pie. **This Victorian recipe for the simplest of pies yields more than you would expect in terms of flavour and versatility. It can be eaten hot (try it next to baked beans!), but somehow it is even better cold. Serve it with good ham or smoked fish, a watercress salad and a couple of pickles. It's good picnic food. Add a bottle of ginger beer and, suddenly, you're part of an Enid Blyton adventure.**

For a greased 20.5cm/8in tin you need:

125g/4oz short crust pastry

250g/9oz potatoes (King Edwards or Elvira are perfect)

125g/4oz butter, chilled and then cut into small cubes

100ml/3½fl oz double cream

1 tbsp of chopped chives

salt and cracked black pepper

First, roll the pastry into two discs, one large enough to line the base and the sides of the cake tin, and one to make the lid. Put the lid piece to one side, the fridge is the best place for it. You can use a floured board, but to make rolling and lining really easy do this:

Sandwich the pastry between two sheets of clingfilm and roll until it is the desired size (and about half a centimeter thick) now gently pull off the top piece of clingfilm and get your hand underneath the other one. Flip the pastry over onto the tin. Gently pull off the clingfilm and press the pastry into the base and sides. If bits of pastry break off or try to go with the clingfilm, just use them to patchwork the base together. With pastry you are like a welder.

Now return the pastry to the fridge or freezer while you work on the filling.

Slice the potatoes as thinly as possible. If you have a gadget like a mandolin then use it. You do not need perfect circular discs so if the potatoes are of any size simply cut them in half before slicing.

Now build the middle of the pie layer by layer. Some of the potato slices, followed by a scattering of chives, butter, salt and pepper, and so on and so on until you have filled the pie.

Put on the lid and press it round to meet the sides. Brush the lid with a little milk or egg to glaze it. Bake the pie at 180°C/350°F/mark 4 for 1 hour and test with a fork to check that the potatoes are cooked. Now make a little nick in the centre of the pie lid (use the end of a teaspoon). Gradually pour in the cream, allowing it to filter down through the strata of potato filling. Let the pie rest for about 15 minutes so that the sides shrink slightly from the cake tin. It should now be easy to take it out. The pie is ready to eat, but save some for that picnic...

Under mash. This section needs no introduction. Mash, used as a pie topping, is as old as the hills. What can be better than breaking open that potato crust to reveal a molten hotch potch of ingredients beneath? They can never cool down fast enough for me and since I was knee high I've been burning my tongue on shepherd's pie and the like.

Shepherd's pie.

The 'true' shepherd's pie is made with minced leftovers from a joint of lamb. The same dish made with beef is really a cottage pie. Few people actually make either using leftovers anymore, and the recipe that follows prescribes fresh mince. For better or worse, the meal is somehow juicier and tastier that way, and few of us have leftovers from a roast come the middle of a busy week. Minced lamb has a stronger flavour than beef, but produces more fat in cooking. I do prefer the flavour of lamb, and there is a way round that fat. I like my shepherd's pie a little on the deep side so I use a baking dish about 20.5cm/8in across and 6.5cm/2½in deep.

For 4 people you need:

1 tsp oil

750g/1lb 10oz minced lamb

1 leek, trimmed and chopped

1 medium onion, chopped

2 medium carrots, diced

1 stick celery, chopped

1 tsp tomato purée

1 tbsp Worcestershire sauce

100ml/3½fl oz stock or water

1 bay leaf

about 750g/1lb 10oz potatoes boiled and then mashed with 4 tbsp milk and 1 tbsp butter

butter for topping

salt and pepper to taste

Preheat the oven to about 200°C/400°F/mark 6.

First, heat a wide-bottomed pan with the oil. Fry the mince hard in this – it will seem very dry at first, but the meat will let go of plenty of fat and juices, which will be used to cook the other ingredients in a minute. When it has browned well, drain the meat over a large bowl, through a colander, catching all the juices.

Keep the meat to one side, but return the juices to the pan. Bubble them fiercely for about a minute before throwing in the leek, onion, carrots and celery. When they have softened (after 10 minutes or so), return the lamb to the pan with the tomato purée and Worcestershire sauce. (These two ingredients may seem a little inauthentic, and of course they are, but you will not register the tomato purée, it works in a very subtle way, and cuts through the lamb's fattiness. The Worcestershire sauce does a similar thing.)

Add the stock or water with the bay leaf and simmer for another 10 minutes or so. Season to taste. Transfer to a casserole or baking dish. Top the pie with the mash and dot it with a little extra butter, if you wish. Bake for 20–25 minutes or until golden and bubbling.

For cottage pie you will need the same weight of minced beef as lamb. You will not find that you need to drain away the fat. Simply set the mince aside after you have browned it and sweat the vegetables in 2 tablespoons of dripping or oil.

(Try shepherd's or cottage pie with the chilli sauce on page 94).

Fish pie. **Traditionally this pie is made with smoked haddock and hard-boiled eggs. I have loosely followed my grandmother's version, adding peas, shrimps and saffron.**

I like to serve this pie, like shepherd's pie, fairly deep. A typical, small casserole (or baking dish), about 20.5cm/8in wide and 6.5cm/2½in deep, is perfect.

For 4 people you need:

2 medium fillets of undyed, smoked haddock (I have always gone by fillet rather than weight since the size of haddock fillets is fairly uniform. The weight of two comes to around 750g/ 1lb 10oz)

1 leek, trimmed, washed and chopped

2 sticks celery, chopped

1 tbsp olive oil

100g/3½oz brown shrimps, or small, peeled prawns

200g/7oz peas (frozen are fine)

a pinch of saffron

a generous pinch of salt

¼ nutmeg, grated

300ml/½ pint water or stock (chicken, ham or fish)

1 tbsp butter

1 heaped tbsp plain flour

3 hard-boiled eggs, peeled and sliced

about 750g/1lb 10oz peeled potatoes, boiled and then mashed with 4 tbsp milk and 1 tbsp butter

Bone and skin the haddock. You could ask the fishmonger to do it, but if not, it is easy: lay the fillet on a chopping board with the tail nearest you. Hold the tail in your left hand. Gently run a sharp knife between the skin and the flesh of the haddock, working from the tail. The meat pulls away easily. Roughly dice and put to one side.

Gently fry the leek and celery in the oil for about 10 minutes. Do not let them brown.

When they are soft add the haddock and the shrimps, then the peas and the seasonings, followed by the water or stock. Bring to the boil, then immediately lower the heat and simmer for about 10 minutes. Now, using a conical sieve or colander over a mixing bowl, strain the fish and vegetables from the liquid. Keep both.

Preheat the oven to 200°C/400°F/mark 6.

Return the pan to the heat. Add the butter and gently heat it. Add the flour and beat it in, as if you were going to make a white sauce. Now add the liquid from the fish, stirring constantly, and cook until it has thickened slightly. This only takes a few minutes. Remove from the heat and mix with the fish, eggs and vegetables.

Pour the whole thing into a deep baking tray or casserole dish. Top with the potatoes and bake for about 25 minutes. Serve when browned on top and bubbling away beneath.

Pacific pie. This is slightly odd (a kind of corned beef hash with tuna). A friend remembered it from childhood and it is a great dish for kids, but it could just as easily have been dreamed up in a student kitchen. The name is gloriously inappropriate since there is very little of the ocean about this dish. No matter, it is almost impossible for you to not have all the ingredients in, making it a good standby supper.

A word about tinned tuna. Even the most tawdry of the supermarkets now seems to have decent options available. Look for Spanish, Portuguese or Italian brands, in olive oil, not brine (cat food in disguise). If you are terrified of the calories you may incur by buying tuna in oil you can always drain the meat thoroughly and even rinse it before using. It is still miles better than the brined stuff.

For 4 hungry people you need:

3 large floury potatoes, peeled and quartered

3 tbsp milk

1 tbsp butter

450g/1lb (a medium tin) good tuna, flaked and drained (keep the oil)

2 medium onions, chopped

400g tin chopped plum tomatoes with their juice

1 tsp sugar

1 tsp red or white wine vinegar

300g/11oz frozen peas, blanched in boiling water, or thawed

1 packet ready-salted crisps, smashed up (this is essential!)

salt and pepper to taste

Boil the potatoes until tender, then drain them well. Mash with the milk and butter and put to one side.

Preheat the oven to 200°C/400°F/mark 6.

Heat the oil from the tuna over a medium flame and fry the onions until they are tender. Do not let them brown.

Add the tomatoes, sugar and vinegar. Add the tuna and simmer for about 10 minutes. Add the peas and remove from the heat. Season carefully with a little salt and maybe pepper.

Transfer the tuna sauce to the bottom of a baking dish and cover with the mashed potatoes, as for a shepherd's pie (see page 98). Cook for 30 minutes.

Just before serving, sprinkle the pie with the smashed crisps. You could whack the oven up to the maximum setting, or place the pie under a grill to brown the new topping, but this is by no means compulsory. Serve with mayonnaise and/or tomato ketchup at the table.

Sussex pie (sort of).

People who are annoyed by inauthentic recipes take note: this is not real or traditional Sussex pie, but a modern, vegetarian spin on it. Times change and things move on. Sussex pie was once the South Downs' shepherd's pie and seems to have been a way of getting around using scrag end or mutton chops. The filling was bulked up by using lentils. Nowadays, when using lentils for bulk is a matter of dietary choice and not economizing on meat, I make this veggie shepherd's pie. I do it because I cannot stand soya mince. You will not find me using it anywhere in the book. Lentils are much better for you anyway. Look for brown lentils (or the increasingly popular lentils du Puy) rather than red or yellow split peas, since these break down when cooked. Even better are the large flat green lentils. And, if you want, by all means add scraps of lamb (or any meat you like) to the vegetables.

Incidentally, the historic topping for this pie was not mash, but slices of potato as it is with Lancashire hot pot (see page 166). Obviously this can be a vegetarian version of that dish, too.

For 4 people you need:

4 tbsp olive oil

2 large onions, peeled and chopped

3 cloves garlic, peeled and chopped

1 sprig of rosemary, chopped

3 sticks celery, washed and chopped

2 carrots, peeled and chopped

200g/7oz lentils

1 litre/1¾ pints vegetable stock

300ml/½ pint bitter (ale)

1 tbsp tomato purée

salt and pepper to taste

about 750g/1lb 10oz peeled potatoes, boiled and then mashed with 4 tbsp milk and 1 tbsp butter

In a large pan, heat 2 tablespoons of the oil and fry the onions, garlic, rosemary, celery and carrots until just about tender. This should take about 15 minutes. Add the lentils to the pot and give the whole thing a stir. Add the stock and beer and simmer for another 30 minutes. After that, check that the lentils are still moist, but soft. If not, add just enough hot water from a kettle to loosen them all up without really covering them. Now keep your eye on them as they are not long off being done. Only when they are cooked should you season them with salt. Adding salt to the cooking liquor for raw pulses toughens them. At this point you can also stir in the tomato purée.

Check the seasoning and, if happy, stir in the last 2 tablespoons of oil. If this seems a little indulgent, it is there to stop the lentils absorbing more liquid, and therefore going stodgy. Truth be told this pie is a little stodgy if left too long anyway, so to get the best results, tip the vegetables straight into a casserole as you would for shepherd's pie (see page 98). Top with the mashed potatoes. If you have a grill and the potatoes are still hot it is a good idea to brown the top of the pie swiftly and tuck in, for the reasons I have just pointed out. That said, no harm is done to the pie by baking it conventionally either.

Some people, me included, still like the taste and texture of lentils that have become a bit 'flumpy'. This pie can be eaten as leftovers and even fried like a hash or bubble and squeak.

M. Noire
Crimée
Carpathes
Budapest
ROUMANIE
Bucarest
HONGRIE
Zagreb
Belgrade
YOUGO SLAVIE
BULGARIE
Istamboul
Salonique
Bursa
Izmir
TURQUIE
Ankara
Konya
Adana
du Taurus
Alep
SYRIE
CHYPRE
Beyrouth
Tel Aviv Jaffa
ISRAËL
Mer Adriatique
Bari
GRÈCE
Athènes
Crète
Marseille
Corse
ROME
Naples
ITALIE
Barcelone
Sardaigne
Palerme
Reggio
Sicile
Malte
MER MÉDITERRANÉE
Alexandrie
Port Saïd
Suez
LE CAIRE
El Fayoum
Madrid
ESPAGNE
Valence
Nevada
Palma
Annaba
Tunis
TUNISIE
Sfax
Gabès
Tripoli
Misurata
Benghazi
Barka
Tobrouk
Marsa Matruh
CYRÉNAÏQUE
Grande Syrte
Alger
Constantine
ALGÉRIE
Chott Djerid
Laghouat
Touggourt
Gibraltar
Tanger
Oran
MAROC
Ghadamès
TRIPOLITAINE
LIBYE
FEZZAN
O. de Koufra
Désert de Libye
ÉGYPTE
(R.A.U.)
SAHARA
Ft. Flatters
Aïn Salah
Adrar
Reggane
OASIS
Ahaggar
Tamanrasset
Mourzouk
Bardaï
Tibesti
O. de Bilma
TCHAD
Largeau
NIGER
Agadès

Around the world. As a nation of eaters we have always been quick to latch onto anything foreign and exciting, so it is hardly surprising that such a wealth of 'foreign food' lines the aisles of even the smallest corner shop. Centuries of intrepid explorers and (lately) scruffy backpackers have contrived to give us very eclectic taste buds.

There was always a thriving trade in exotic foods. It started with spices and grains, the kind of thing that wouldn't perish in the hold of a ship. Today, anything and everything can be transported in the blink of an eye. But before supermarkets were vast international arenas of ingredients, necessity was the mother of invention: you improvised. Ideas were shared and methods became literally tried and tested.

Cooking is a game of Chinese whispers and soon many of these dishes became unrecognizable in the lands where they originated. Curry is in many respects Anglo-Indian. When it was recently claimed that chicken tikka masala was now a British favourite, what was being referred to was the hybrid dish that always shared more ancestry with the Midlands than the Punjab. What you find over here may have never happened over there. It hardly matters anymore since the two cuisines are so bound up with one another. The buzz word these days is authenticity since the modern cook is now wise to vast regional variations in the cookery of the sub-continent. Cookery writers like Madhur Jaffrey have revolutionized the way we prepare Indian food at home and retailers have risen to the challenge of ensuring that her disciples need not undertake an epic pilgrimage to find what they need.

Equally, in 21st-century Britain anything remotely Mediterranean is big business and pasta, for many people, is the last word in Italian food. Adherents to the current craze for low-carb diets may suddenly regard it with suspicion but I doubt that supermarkets, with their aisles full of tubes and ribbons, are worried yet. Everything you need for the latest Jamie Oliver recipe is staring you in the face. It wasn't always so. I can still remember a time when Parmesan was a very scary, dried cheese and no-one knew what 'al dente' meant. The following recipes are from that time. They are the kind of dishes that started out exotic and got clumsily Anglicized to the point where they became comforting and familiar. Don't worry! You won't need to boil your pasta to a pulp or hunt down the world's worst curry powder to make them. This chapter is not about yearning for a culinary time gone by but it is worth noting that, with everything available to us, we may have lost a little of our inventive streak.

A curry lunch. **This recipe was my grandfather's. He delighted in serving it to a large crowd for Sunday lunch in the days when curry was just curry, something otherworldly and exotic. It would be easy to write off this recipe as inauthentic, but what my grandfather created was actually something just as worthy. It was inventive. He took the time to prepare his own curry powder, but when he couldn't find something he improvised. I never got round to asking him why he put marmalade in the pot, but possibly it was there in place of a souring agent that he couldn't get hold of. His home-made marmalades were sharp because he didn't eat sugary food. I find shop-bought marmalade too sweet for this recipe so I use a lime, cut up and cooked with the other ingredients.**

You can use whatever meat you like for the curry. Pork would be unheard of in most of India but it works well. If you want to make it without meat I recommend a mixture of potato, peppers, something like cauliflower and a sturdy pulse like chickpeas. A vegetable curry will cook in about a third of the time of a meat version. Do not serve this without the garnishes, which make the meal.

For 4 people you need:
3 tbsp butter
1kg/2½lb diced beef or lamb
2 medium onions, chopped
2 cloves garlic, chopped
2cm/¾in piece fresh ginger, peeled and chopped
400g tin tomatoes, drained
2 tsp salt
1 tsp brown sugar
1 tbsp tomato purée
1 tbsp marmalade, or 1 lime, roughly diced

My grandfather's curry powder – combine the following ingredients:
4 tbsp ground coriander
2 tbsp ground cumin
1 tbsp turmeric powder
1 tsp ground chilli or cayenne pepper
1 tsp cinnamon
¼ tsp grated nutmeg
2 cloves, crushed
6 cardamom pods, crushed

Heat the butter in a large pot or casserole and when it is hot, brown all the meat in batches and remove with a slotted spoon.

Add the onions, garlic and ginger to the pot with 2 tablespoons of the curry powder and fry all the ingredients over a medium heat for about 15 minutes, stirring occasionally. It's okay for the onions to catch a little.

Next, stir in the tomatoes, salt, sugar and tomato purée and turn the heat up high. Add the meat, 300ml/½ pint of water and the marmalade or lime. Allow the curry to come to a simmer then lower the heat and cook, covered, for at least 2 hours. Keep an eye on the liquid, and if it is looking dry add a little more water. If the curry is not thickening at all (it depends on the pot really) remove the lid and raise the heat a little near the end of the cooking time. The dish is ready when the meat is really tender and the juices are glossy. Check the seasoning before serving.

The garnishes. At my grandfather's table there were always bowls of ingredients to put with the curry. They were desiccated coconut, sliced bananas, sliced cucumbers, peanuts and shop-bought mango chutney or lime pickle. Sometimes there was yoghurt, too. These all added to the lavish sense of occasion and should not be overlooked, no matter how old-fashioned they seem now.

Polynesian pork chops. **Two dishes that married pork with pineapple to evoke the balmy atmosphere of some corner of Micronesia stand out in my memory. One is the truly horrendous 'Hawaiian Steak', which was served with alarming regularity at my school. As far as I can remember it was a piece of gammon grilled with a ring of tinned pineapple on the top. The insipid piece of fruit absorbed all the salt from the gammon in the process, rendering it almost pointless. This crime against both fruit and pig still languishes on the odd pizza today and should be avoided at all costs. The second dish was far better. It was a real sweet-n-sour affair. It is probably about as Tahitian as a Bounty bar but you should try it anyway.**

You could use pork loin chops for this, but it is better with the fattier cut from the belly. Double the braising time if you go for that. You want the meat and the fat on a pork belly chop to be very tender.

For 4 people you need:

2 tbsp lard (pork fat), or olive oil

4 large pork chops

1 medium onion, sliced

2 cloves garlic, sliced

2cm/½in piece fresh ginger, peeled and chopped

2 green peppers, cored, seeded and sliced

1 tsp salt

200ml/7fl oz wine or cider vinegar

1 level tbsp tomato or red pepper purée

1 level tbsp brown sugar, or honey

400g tin pineapple pieces in their own juice

Heat the lard or oil in a large casserole or pot and brown the pork chops on both sides. Remove them from the pan and throw in the onions, garlic, ginger and peppers. Add the salt and stir it through. Lower the heat, cover and leave the vegetables to sweat for about 10 minutes, stirring them only occasionally.

Turn the heat back up and add the vinegar, tomato or pepper purée and sugar. Allow everything to bubble fiercely for a couple of minutes. Now lay the chops back onto the vegetables and add the pineapple pieces with all their juice, plus 200ml/7fl oz of water. Cover and simmer very gently for about 1½ hours or until the meat is tender. Serve this with plenty of slightly sticky rice.

Chilli con carne. **Whether or not any of us has ever contemplated it, to eat a plate of chilli con carne (literally 'meat with chilli pepper') is to taste the roots of a seismic shift in the world's eating habits. The chilli pepper is native to Central and Latin America. It was unknown to the rest of the world before the Spanish and Portuguese arrived there and then the Portuguese introduced chilli peppers to Africa and Asia, where they became an integral part of spice pastes and powders. Before the chilli made its long journey eastwards, the 'heat' in oriental food came from peppercorns (a different type of plant altogether). Had the colonists and explorers never eaten chilli, all the modern-day 'hot' food of India and Thailand might taste entirely different. (Thailand was never colonized, but the neighbouring Malay peninsula was. Malacca, in modern-day Malaysia, still bears the hallmarks of its old Portuguese masters.)**

Chilli con carne is Mexican. Surprisingly, beans are not an authentic addition, but a 'chilli' without beans would be unrecognizable to most people. The recipe that follows is my favourite version.

For 4 people you need:

200g/7oz dried red kidney or pinto beans, soaked overnight, or 400g tin red kidney or pinto beans, with all the stock

5 cloves garlic

2 bay leaves

5 tbsp olive oil

500g/1lb 2oz minced beef

2 medium onions, finely chopped

1 green pepper, roughly chopped

2 fresh red chillies, chopped (reduce or increase this for your desired heat)

½ tsp smoked paprika (optional. If you have unsmoked use that)

1 tbsp salt

400g tin plum tomatoes, squashed and drained

1 tbsp tomato purée

First, deal with the beans if using dried. Put them in a saucepan with 2 litres/3½ pints of water and bring them to a rolling boil. Boil hard for 10 minutes, skimming off any froth that rises to the surface, then drain them completely and rinse with cold water. Put back into the pan with the same amount of water, 2 of the whole garlic cloves and the bay leaves. Bring to the boil then simmer gently. The cooking time of the beans will depend on their age, but they will take at least 1 hour. Keep an eye on the water level, which should always be a good half a finger higher than the beans. When the hour is up, taste a bean to see how it is. You want them creamy, but not falling to bits. When the beans are done put them to one side, in their stock.

Heat the oil in a wide pot or casserole and brown the mince thoroughly. Remove it with a slotted spoon and set aside. Finely chop the remaining garlic cloves and add to the pan with the onions, green pepper and chillies for a minute or so on a fairly high heat then add the paprika and salt. Stir once, lower the heat, cover the pan and let the vegetables 'sweat' for about 15 minutes. Check them now and again to make sure they are not catching.

Now add the meat, tomatoes, tomato purée and as many of the cooked or tinned beans, with some of their stock, as you want. The stew can be very beany or very meaty. Simmer all the ingredients together for about 30 minutes and check the seasoning again before serving. I love to serve chilli con carne with rice or tortilla (the bread-like kind that are used to make wraps). Sour cream at the table is lovely if people want to add it. I make no apology if all the above sounds a bit 'tex mex', because it is!

Coq au vin. ***Coq*** **is the French word for rooster. No farmer in his right mind would kill off a male bird until he was too old to breed, so by the time the old boy made it into the pot he might be pretty long in the tooth, and tough to eat. Coq au Vin, with its long, slow cooking time, was originally a way round this problem. The quintessential French casserole is now made with chicken, of course.**

You could buy a largish hen and quarter it, but you might face arguments about who eats the leg and who gets the breast. I must admit that I think legs make the best braising cuts on all poultry, so I would buy them. The other option and one I increasingly turn to is to use whole poussin (spring chickens). Give everyone an entire bird and the casserole looks marvellous. As I have said before, you must buy free-range chicken for flavour as much as for anything else.

For 4 people you need:

- 3 tbsp olive oil
- 100g/3½oz unsmoked streaky bacon, roughly diced
- 4 large chicken legs, or 8 spring chickens (poussin)
- 300g/11oz small shallots, peeled and left whole
- 6 cloves garlic, peeled and left whole
- 2 sticks celery, each one cut into about 4 pieces
- 1 sprig of rosemary, or thyme (or both)
- 3 bay leaves
- 50ml/2fl oz cooking brandy
- 500ml/17fl oz red wine
- 8 field mushrooms, washed and left whole (you could use any mushroom you like really)
- 1 litre/1¾ pints chicken stock or water
- 2 tsp salt
- 1 tbsp unsalted butter

Heat the olive oil fairly swiftly in a large casserole or pot and fry the bacon quite hard. Lift it out with a slotted spoon after about 5 minutes and set aside. Leave as much fat as you can in the pot.

Next, brown the chicken pieces (or poussin) and remove them. Now fry the shallots and garlic until they have 'caught' a bit. Return everything you have cooked so far to the pot and throw in the celery and herbs. Keep the heat high and pour in the brandy. Set light to it if you wish or wait a minute for the alcohol to evaporate. Add the wine and the mushrooms and let the wine bubble fiercely for 2 minutes. Now add the stock or water and the salt and simmer gently for about 1½ hours, covered.

Just before serving, drop in the butter, replace the lid and shake the pot very gently so that it emulsifies with the liquids within. Check the seasoning before you serve, and add more salt if you need to.

Note that I do not thicken coq au vin. The received wisdom on this is to dip the chicken pieces in flour before you brown them. I like my chicken casseroles a touch brothy so I never do this.

You could serve this casserole over pasta, like tagliatelle, or rice. It is also delicious with mash or something as basic as crusty bread.

My mum's beef stroganoff. **Beef stroganoff is either a Russian or French invention, depending on how you look at it. The Stroganoffs were nobles who lived at the turn of the 18th century. At least one of the branches of the family employed a French chef who might have named the dish after his masters. Either that or he learned it from them. It is thought of as a Russian classic by most people today. This is not the haute cuisine version of stroganoff, where fillet steak is served with sautéed mushrooms and sour cream, but a homely version we ate when I was little. It is slow cooked shin of beef which makes it very affordable. Serve this over rice.**

For 4 people you need:

50g/2oz butter

700g/1½lb diced shin or leg of beef (or ask the butcher for his best stewing steak)

2 medium onions, finely chopped

450g/1lb button mushrooms, roughly sliced

1 hefty tbsp tomato purée

750ml/1¼ pints chicken stock (or water and a beef stock cube)

250g/9oz soured cream (crème fraîche will do if it is easier to get hold of)

salt and pepper to taste

Heat the butter in a large pot or casserole and brown the beef in batches. Set the meat to one side.

Add the onions to the pot and stir to coat them in the remaining fat and juices.

Cook them over a medium heat for about 5 minutes then add the mushrooms, tomato purée and the meat. Stir everything together and add the stock.

Add half the soured cream and simmer, covered for at least 1½ hours. You want the beef to be really tender. The soured cream will help tenderize it a little, but taste it at this point. It might need as much as 2 hours so keep cooking. When the meat is tender and to your liking, season the stew. If it looks too liquid, raise the heat and, stirring constantly, boil to reduce it for a few minutes. Just before serving add the remaining soured cream and check the seasoning one more time.

Aubergines. Although the aubergine will grow quite comfortably in a greenhouse or a sunny corner, it has always been seen as a truly exotic vegetable. Certainly, I cannot think of any aubergine dish that could be described as native to Britain. Not everyone likes aubergine and I think this is due to our collective ignorance about how it should be cooked. There is one golden rule here and that is that it should never go into a stew or baked dish in its raw state. Absolutely every dish I know of with aubergine calls for it to be roasted or fried on its own first.

The most common type of aubergine seen in our shops is the large, dark, oval-shaped kind. If you come across the paler, Italian variety do try them. They have a creamier taste, but won't give you that jet black, glossy skin that looks so appealing in, say, a ratatouille.

Smoked aubergine purée

(or baba ganoush). This is just a quick aubergine dip that can be served on toast or with grilled pitta bread and I include it merely as a ruse to try and convert the most fervent aubergine haters amongst us (they seem to be legion). You may or may not wish to include the tahini (sesame paste), which can be found just about everywhere now due to the popularity of hummus, of which it is a central ingredient.

For 4 people (as a starter) you need:

1 or 2 aubergines (1 large one will do)

2 cloves garlic

2 tbsp extra virgin olive oil

½ tsp salt

¼ tsp freshly ground black pepper

1 tbsp tahini

juice of 1 lemon

The first part is easier if you have a gas hob. Prick the aubergine with a fork and blacken it over a high flame. This takes about 2 minutes on each side. The aubergine will go soft as it blackens. If you don't have a gas ring cook the aubergine in the oven for about 20 minutes on full whack. Check it after that time; it should be soft and wrinkly.

Allow the aubergine to cool completely in a bowl covered with a plate or lid or some clingfilm. This helps the skin steam itself loose.

Pull the skin off the cooled aubergine and discard, along with the stalk.

Now put all the remaining ingredients into a food processor with the aubergine and blitz them until smooth. If the purée looks too thick, loosen it with a little more oil. If it looks too loose add another half spoonful of tahini. Check the seasoning and rest it for 30 minutes before serving (it will thicken a little as it cools further).

Moussaka. **The famous lamb and aubergine gratin from Greece was once much more common than it is today. It went out of style because it was remembered as a very oily concoction, and it is, but that can be got round. One way is to grill or roast the Aubergines rather than frying them in oil. The other greasy element of moussaka is the lamb itself, which releases its own fat as it cooks, but this needn't be a problem if you follow the method below.**

For 4 people you need:

oil for greasing

450g/1lb minced lamb, as lean as possible

2 medium onions, finely chopped

4 cloves garlic, chopped

400g tin plum tomatoes, squished and drained

1 glass (approx 150ml/ ¼ pint) red wine

1 cinnamon stick, or 1 level tsp ground cinnamon

2 bay leaves

2 medium aubergines, sliced into rounds about 1cm/½in thick

a fairly generous slug of olive oil

1 level tsp salt

salt and freshly ground black pepper to taste

The béchamel-type sauce:

2 eggs, separated

1 generous tbsp flour

500ml/17fl oz milk

25g/1oz freshly grated gruyère or Parmesan cheese

¼ nutmeg, grated

½ tsp salt

Preheat the oven to 200°C/400°F/gas 6. Grease a fairly deep casserole or baking dish.

Heat a wide-bottomed pan without fat and when it is searingly hot add the lamb. Brown well, then remove it with a slotted spoon. Leave any liquid that has accumulated in the pan. Lower the heat, add the onions and garlic and sauté them for about 5 minutes or until they begin to soften. Add the meat, tomatoes, wine, cinnamon, bay leaves and seasoning, then cover and simmer for about 30 minutes.

While the lamb cooks, put the aubergine slices into a mixing bowl and drizzle them with enough oil to coat them all lightly. Toss them with the teaspoon of salt and lay them on a baking tray. You may have been told to salt aubergines and leave them in a colander for a while to remove the bitter juices, but these will evaporate if you roast them so there is no need. Cook them in the oven this way until they are soft to the touch and dark around the edges. Allow them to cool on the tray.

Now make the sauce. Beat the egg yolks and flour until smooth and pale. Heat the milk in a small pan until it reaches scalding point (it will fizz against the side of the pan). Pour about a third over the yolks and whisk until incorporated. Pour over the rest and whisk again. Pour into the pan, return to the heat and cook gently, stirring constantly, until the sauce coats the back of the spoon. Take off the heat and fold in the cheese, nutmeg and salt.

Put half the meat mixture into the casserole or dish. Cover with half the aubergine slices and then the remaining meat. Top with the remaining aubergine slices.

Then finish off the sauce. Whisk the egg whites until they form soft peaks then fold them into the cheese sauce. Pour this over the moussaka and bake for about 25 minutes or until the top is golden brown. Serve immediately.

Serve with good bread and a side salad.

Ratatouille with baked eggs.

Baking eggs with ratatouille is possibly a hybrid of a less well-known French dish called pipérade, where eggs are added to braised peppers, and I can't sell this to you without admitting that it sounds odd. Do have a go, you will be smitten. Not only does it make ratatouille a nourishing, complete veggie meal, it is also a soothing, autumnal supper. It is best saved for the last of those warm days when aubergines, courgettes and the like seem appropriate fare. Look out for huge Spanish or Italian peppers and try to eschew the stingy little versions grown under glass in the European winter. The same applies to aubergines.

Good ratatouille is made by cooking the vegetables separately from one another and the easiest way to do that is to roast the aubergines and courgettes whilst braising the peppers. Tomatoes (I always use tinned since they are effortless and flavoursome) should be added later. If all these instructions sound a touch ardent don't worry, the whole thing is a cinch.

For 4 people you need:

2 aubergines (or 1 large one), very roughly diced

2 courgettes, diced like the aubergine

olive oil

1 large or two medium onions, chopped

6 cloves garlic, just bruised (that is to say, squashed a bit with the flat side of your knife. Chop them up if you really want to)

1 red pepper and 1 green pepper, roughly chopped (or 2 red if you prefer)

1 tbsp wine or balsamic vinegar

1 tsp sugar

a handful or sprig of chopped herbs (what you use is up to you but in the summer basil is wonderful. In the winter I like thyme)

1 bay leaf

400g tin peeled plum tomatoes, juice drained and reserved

salt and freshly ground black pepper to taste

8 eggs

Heat the oven to 200°C/400°F/mark 6 and pop in two small roasting trays.

Season the aubergines and courgettes with a slug of olive oil and a pinch of salt. Transfer each to a roasting tray and bake for 30 minutes or so. Check them halfway through. If you have a fierce beast of an oven like me they may cook quicker.

Meanwhile, heat 2 tablespoons of olive oil in a large pan or casserole. Add the onions, garlic and peppers, stir round a few times, cover the pan and lower the heat. Braise them, stirring from time to time, until soft and juicy.

Drain the aubergines and courgettes of any juices and keep to one side. When the peppers and onions are cooked, add the vinegar, sugar, herbs (unless you have opted for basil, in which case add it at the end), bay leaf and tomatoes. Bring the heat up until they are simmering and cook gently, uncovered, until the tomatoes are looking darker and stickier. If it looks dry or as if it might catch, add some of the tomato juice. Add the aubergines and courgettes and cook for another 5 minutes. Season to taste. It should be sweet and sourish, with a good salty note.

To bake all of the above with eggs, use individual terracotta or enamel bowls. If you are in possession of a balti-style metal bowl it will also do the trick. Otherwise do the whole thing in a baking dish and serve carefully, avoiding breaking the yolks. While the ratatouille is still hot, half-fill each dish, make a rough well in the middle of each and break 2 eggs into each well. Season each egg with a pinch of black pepper and slam in the oven for about 10–15 minutes. The meal is ready when the eggs are as done as you like them. Needless to say a runny yolk is unbeatable here.

Macaroni cheese.

How Italian is this dish? It is hard to tell. Anglo-Italian perhaps (in the way that kedgeree and mulligatawny are sort of Indian). Macaroni (or *maccherone*) is really the name for a whole group of hollow pasta shapes. In some parts of southern Italy the word refers to hundreds of variations. Here it tends to be a small, slightly curled tube. Macaroni cheese is possibly a hybrid of any number of pasta 'gratins'. The sauce is something like béchamel in its simplest form, and simplicity is the key to macaroni cheese really. Nothing should leap out at you except a clumsy, gooey richness.

When fresh Parmesan became more widely available in British shops lots of people ditched the old habit of adding Cheddar to the sauce. I think we all felt we ought to! We were missing the point of macaroni cheese. There should be a bit of stringy trail between the spoon and the dish when you lift this to your mouth. If you want to use an Italian cheese look for something like fontina instead of Parmesan.

For 4 people you need:

50g/2oz butter, plus extra for greasing

50g/2oz plain flour

800m/1¼ pints whole milk

50g/2oz freshly grated matured Cheddar (or fontina) cheese

400g/14oz macaroni pasta

3 plum tomatoes, sliced, or a handful of cherry tomatoes left whole (optional)

salt and pepper to taste

My mother always tops this dish with tomatoes so that they get a bit of a grilling with the cheese. You can omit them if you like.

Preheat the oven to the highest setting (or if it has a grill facility use that). Rub the base and sides of a fairly deep baking dish with a little butter and set aside.

Heat about 3 litres/5¼ pints of generously salted water in the largest pan you have.

Meanwhile, heat the butter on a medium heat in a pan and when it is bubbling gently throw in the flour and stir vigorously until you have a fairly stiff paste. Keep stirring for another minute or so, over the heat. Add about a third of the milk and keep stirring. If you are worried about lumps at this point use a whisk. Add the rest of the milk and cook for a few more minutes. As soon as the sauce starts to thicken fold in two-thirds of the cheese. When the cheese has melted, season to taste and set aside with a lid on.

When the pan of water is at a rolling boil, throw in the macaroni and stir several times to prevent it hiding at the bottom and sticking. Cook the pasta until it is as tender as you like it. For macaroni cheese you do not need to worry about al dente pasta, it is more about gooey tenderness. As soon as the pasta is done to your liking drain it and fold into the cheese sauce. Pop it into the baking dish and dot the top with the remaining cheese, the tomatoes (if using) and a pinch of freshly ground black pepper. Bake the macaroni until the top has grilled nicely, and then serve.

Lasagne. **Or, to be pedantic, lasagne al forno, since lasagne is the name of the pasta and al forno means literally 'in the oven'. This was always dinner party pasta, but now that it is such a part of our lives it's become a very homely affair. There are actually lots of versions of lasagne al forno but the classic one uses the Bolognese-style sauce (see page 120 but omit the mushrooms) with a pretty simple béchamel.**

For 4 people you need:

approx. 250g/9oz (or half a box) lasagne al uovo

1 quantity Bolognese sauce (see page 120)

The béchamel:

75g/3oz unsalted butter, plus extra for greasing

50g/2oz plain flour

600ml/1 pint milk

50g/2oz freshly grated Parmesan cheese

½ nutmeg, grated

½ tsp salt

¼ tsp freshly ground black pepper

These days most shop-bought lasagne needs no pre-boiling, but you can reduce the cooking time by dunking each sheet in rapidly boiling water and laying it out between two damp tea towels. The green stuff, by the way, is one of the most pointless things ever invented and tastes the same as the white.

Preheat the oven to 200°C/400°F/mark 6. Grease the bottom and sides of your favourite baking dish.

Make up the Bolognese sauce and then make the béchamel. Heat the butter and when it is bubbling gently add the flour. Stir it into the butter until you have the beginnings of a paste. Let the paste cook, stirring constantly, for about 1 minute then gradually start to add the milk. It will thicken fairly quickly. If you are worried about lumps use a whisk to stir it. When the sauce has thickened add two-thirds of the Parmesan and the seasonings and put to one side.

Now, with the 2 sauces ready (they should both be hot), you layer the dish. How you do it is up to you and the baking dish, but traditionally you start with a layer of the Bolognese sauce, then the pasta, then the béchamel, and so on. I like my lasagne to have at least two layers of pasta (ideally three) and the top layer should just be covered with the last of the béchamel and Parmesan. This way the pasta gets a bit crispy round the edges.

If the pasta is raw leave all the ingredients to get to know each other in the dish for 20 minutes and then bake the dish for a good 30 minutes, or until it is golden brown on top. If you dipped the pasta you can omit the 20-minute rest before cooking.

A decent vegetarian lasagne.

In Italy, there are probably more versions of lasagne without meat than there are with. By far the best is one made with a simple tomato and spinach sauce. I would omit the béchamel and season a good ricotta cheese instead.

For 4 people you need:

approx. 250g/9oz (or half a box) lasagne al uovo

The tomato sauce:

4 tbsp olive oil, plus extra for greasing

4 cloves garlic, chopped

2 medium onions, chopped

1 tsp salt

3 tins plum tomatoes, drained of all juice (squish them into a colander with your hands so that all you have is the pulp)

1 tbsp wine or balsamic vinegar

½ tsp sugar

1kg/2¼lb spinach, washed and picked

a handful of basil or parsley

The cheese sauce:

500g/1lb 2oz ricotta cheese

1 whole egg plus 1 egg yolk

50g/2oz Parmesan cheese

100ml/3½fl oz milk

¼ nutmeg grated

1 tsp salt

½ tsp freshly ground black pepper

First make the tomato sauce. Heat the olive oil in a wide-bottomed saucepan. Add the garlic and onions and fry them for about 1 minute, then really lower the heat. Throw in the salt and stir once. Cover the pan and leave to sweat for about 10 minutes. Add the tomatoes, vinegar and sugar and simmer the sauce gently for about 40 minutes. Stir from time to time to prevent it sticking. Keep the heat nice and low.

Meanwhile, blanch the spinach. Heat a saucepan of water to a rolling boil and literally 'dunk' the spinach for about 20 seconds. You might have to do it in a couple of batches unless the pan is nice and big. Cool the spinach and squeeze out any excess liquid. You can wring it with your hands once cool enough, or put a weight on it in a colander. As soon as it is nice and dry chop it finely like a herb and add it to the tomato sauce with the basil or parsley.

Now make the cheese sauce. Put the ricotta, eggs and two-thirds of the Parmesan into a bowl and stir in the milk, little by little, until you have a smooth paste. When it feels loose and plentiful enough to cover two layers of pasta, season it with the nutmeg, salt and pepper.

Preheat the oven to 200°C/400°F/mark 6. Grease the bottom and sides of your favourite baking dish. These days most shop-bought lasagne needs no pre-boiling but you can reduce the cooking time by dipping each sheet in rapidly boiling water for about 30 seconds and laying it between two damp tea towels.

With both sauces ready (the tomato sauce should still be warm), you layer the dish. How you do it is up to you and the baking dish really but traditionally you start with a layer of the tomato sauce, then the pasta, then the ricotta, and so on. I like my lasagne to have at least two layers of pasta (ideally three) and the top layer should just be covered with the last of the ricotta and Parmesan. This way the pasta gets a bit crispy round the edges.

If the pasta is raw leave all the ingredients to get to know each other in the dish for 20 minutes, then bake in the oven for a good 30 minutes, or until it is golden brown on top.

Spaghetti Bolognese. **My grandmother was the first pasta chef in our family. Once my father and his brothers were old enough to frequent the pubs she found that a huge plate of 'spag bol' was a useful way of ensuring that they could only manage about half a lager. This is not the definitive spaghetti alla Bolognese by any stretch of the imagination. In Emilio Romagna, where this originates, it is traditional to use a mixture of minced pork and veal. We never ate veal in my family, probably due to the expense, and I tend to make it with pork and bacon these days.**

For 4 people (who won't be going on a pub crawl later) you need:

3 tbsp olive oil, or a similar quantity of lard (pork fat)

2 cloves garlic, finely chopped

1 medium onion, finely chopped

1 stick celery, very finely chopped

1 large carrot, very finely chopped

1 tsp salt (and extra to taste)

50g/2oz unsmoked pancetta, or good-quality streaky bacon, cut into small slivers

200g/7oz minced pork (or veal or beef, or half and half)

1 tbsp tomato purée, or 3 tbsp passata

2 glasses red wine

200ml/7fl oz water or chicken stock

2 generous tbsp unsalted butter

500g packet of good-quality spaghetti – buy an Italian brand

Optional extras:

3 or 4 field mushrooms, roughly chopped

50g/2oz freshly grated Parmesan cheese

Successful spaghetti Bolognese means having the sauce well and truly ready before you think about the pasta. There is no reason why you couldn't make this a good day in advance since the flavour will intensify. In fact you could double up the quantities and freeze some.

Gently heat the olive oil or lard in a large pan and add the garlic, onion, celery and carrot. Fry them for about 1 minute, then really lower the heat. Throw in the teaspoon of salt and stir once. Cover the pan and leave the vegetables to sweat for about 10 minutes. After 10 minutes add the bacon, then 5 minutes later add the mince and when it has browned fully stir in the tomato purée or passata.

Add the wine and turn the heat up until it bubbles fiercely. Let this go on for a minute or so then add the water or stock. If you want mushrooms add them now. Let the stock come up to a simmer and lower the heat again so that you can cook the sauce gently for about 1½ hours. When the sauce is ready stir in the butter and check the seasoning. Rest the sauce on one side, off the heat.

Now for the pasta. To cook pasta well, without angst, use lots of salted water, in your biggest pot. For a 500g/1lb 2oz packet of spaghetti you want about 4 litres/7 pints of water, if your pan is big enough. Forget everything anyone ever said about adding oil to the water, it's nonsense. You just want the water to be at a really rolling boil. Lower the spaghetti in and fan it out with the end of a spoon. Keep moving it around at first to prevent it sticking. The cooking time will be around 10 minutes, but taste a piece before you drain it to see if it is to your liking. Much has been said about 'al dente' pasta, which just means that it still has some 'bite' to it without having gone soggy. Drain the pasta when you feel it is ready and toss it round a bowl with a little more butter or olive oil. This will stop it sticking while you transfer it to people's bowls.

To serve the traditional way spoon the sauce over the pasta.

A grain of rice. Rice is the basic staple of well over half the world's population. Whole civilizations have grown up around its meticulous cultivation and many people's day-to-day lives still revolve around the vast scale of its production and consumption. A meal without rice would be unthinkable in south-east Asia. The Cantonese for 'have you eaten?' is 'sek fan?', which literally translates as 'have you had rice?'.

For us, rice is a curious mix of the truly exotic and the comfortingly familiar. Nothing could be more thrillingly alien than the image of a terraced paddy field framed by a monsoon sky, or a pilaf studded with dried fruits and strands of saffron. Yet few things beat rice pudding for emitting a sense of English nursery food.

Rice has been eaten in Britain for centuries. It was first imported as a spice, and then it developed a reputation as a medicinal food. This was based on wisdom rather than misconception. Rice is good for an upset stomach and a delicate constitution. It is one of the few foods in the world that you cannot be allergic to and the delicate, white grains have an aura of cleanliness and purity about them. Few people, faced with their first helping of rice, would eye it up with suspicion. It may come from far away, but there is something reassuring about the way it looks and tastes.

Quite apart from that, it is nourishing and delicious. It is also very versatile. The many different varieties behave in their own way when cooked, so that a rice-based dish can be sticky, creamy, fluffy or toothsome, depending on what you're after.

The following recipes are here to show you a fraction of this versatility. I hope they will reflect the dual role of rice in our lives as something exotic and homely all at once.

For texture, reliability and flavour, I only ever buy one type of long-grained rice: basmati. The name literally means 'fragrant' because it has a distinct, slightly nutty perfume, which just comes through to you as you eat it. It is only grown in the Himalayan foothills so we are talking about a very specific kind of rice (but luckily one that is widely available in this country). It is a little pricier than some long-grained rice, but worth every extra penny

Quite apart from its superior taste, basmati behaves very well. Unlike most rice, it elongates rather than swells during cooking so it needs to be handled gently. These days you do not need to wash most brands before cooking, but there are rules to follow to get the best results.

Perfectly cooked rice. I should just say here that if you eat a lot of rice it is worth buying a small, electric rice cooker. They are the best culinary invention of all time. You simply measure out how much rice you need and add the same amount of water (all this is done with the handy little plastic beaker you get with a rice cooker). Then you pop on the lid and switch it on. After an indecently short interlude the rice cooker clicks itself off, having produced perfect fluffy grains for you. How does it do this? Well, it's not magic, although that would be nice. The cooker apes the Asian-wide method of cooking rice by water absorption, and this is easy, too.

You need a pan with a tight-fitting lid and a dose of confidence. Measure out the rice – a healthy portion for one person is 150g/5oz, but doing this by sight is better than weight. If you own an espresso-sized coffee cup (or the American ½ cup measuring spoon) fill it to the brim. To cook that by absorption in a pan you add exactly 1½ times the amount of cold water to rice.

Bring the water to the brink of boiling then lower the heat as much as you can. You want the water to barely simmer (think of a breeze ruffling the surface of a pond). Fit the lid snugly and cook the rice this way for about 12 minutes. When all the water has been absorbed fluff the rice with a fork or a skewer, but not a spoon (it will smash the grains). Let it rest off the heat for a couple of minutes and then it is ready to serve.

A simple rice salad.

When I was small, long car journeys had to be punctuated by a picnic stop. It was always rice salad and a pile of chicken drumsticks, all neatly set out in plastic boxes. The preparations for these car safaris must have been so thorough and yet none of the industriousness has rubbed off on me. Every time I end up eating a sandwich in a service station I could kick myself.

For 4 people you need:

200g/7oz basmati rice (to give you about 450g/1lb cooked weight)

100g/3½oz flaked almonds

25g/1oz pine nuts

1 tbsp soft butter

1 tsp whole cumin seeds

1cm/½in piece fresh ginger, peeled and chopped

50g/2oz dried apricots

125g/4oz sultanas, or pale raisins, soaked in water until soft, then squeezed dry

3 spring onions, finely sliced

a generous bunch of flat-leafed parsley, roughly chopped

juice of 1 lemon

3 generous tbsp extra virgin olive oil

salt and pepper to taste

First cook the rice – follow the instructions for cooking long-grain rice above and allow the rice to cool for about 15 minutes. You can make the salad with hot rice, but if you do, leave the parsley and spring onions as a garnish.

Combine the almonds and pine nuts in a mixing bowl.

In the smallest pan you can find, heat the butter and throw in the cumin and ginger. Lower the heat and fry them just enough to unlock the flavour – it takes about 1 minute. Throw the butter and spices over the nuts and stir them together.

In another bowl, combine the dried fruit, spring onions, parsley, lemon juice and olive oil. Start to add the rice, bit by bit, and fold each lot in. I say this because you might not want all the rice. The salad can be as green or as 'ricey' as you like. Finally, toss in the nuts. Season when you have the combination you want.

Kedgeree. **Kedgeree is the Anglicized version of an Indian dish (*kichiri*) of rice cooked with lentils and spices in one pot. How it ended up containing smoked fish is anyone's guess although it may have had something to do with the East India Company's relationship with the city of Calcutta. Fish and seafood are well represented in Bengali cuisine. However it evolved, kedgeree is a wonderful thing: a great lunch or indeed, breakfast. It has a history of being served in the wee hours at the end of decadent, night-long parties in Colonial clubs and officers' messes. Again, quite why remains a bit of a mystery, but it must have been a great comfort to the exhausted guests.**

Kedgeree should taste smoky and spicy all at once. Neither fish nor curry powder should outdo the other. I use a mild curry powder rather than the fierce Madras kind. You must use curry powder, by the way. If you want to make my grandfather's home-made kind see page 106.

Since this dish is, itself, evolved, I will give you my version. It might depart from 'historical' kedgeree but surely that's the spirit of the thing?

For 4 people you need:

3 tbsp soft butter

1 large onion, finely chopped

1 level tbsp curry powder

100g/3½oz peas (thawed, if frozen)

500g/1lb 2oz smoked haddock (i.e. 1 large fillet), skinned, boned and diced

1 level tsp salt

300g/11oz basmati rice

3 hard-boiled eggs, chopped

a handful of parsley, roughly chopped

Heat 1 tablespoon of the butter in a wide-bottomed saucepan and fry the onion, fairly gently, for a good 5–10 minutes. It should be nice and soft. When this is the case, add the curry powder, peas, fish and salt.

Lower the heat so that it is very gentle and cover the pan with a lid. Let the ingredients sweat for a further 10 minutes and then remove them to a bowl.

Add the rice to the used pan and pour on 400ml/14fl oz of water. Stir just once and raise the heat. As soon as the water starts to fizz against the side of the pan lower the heat again. Cover the rice and simmer very gently, undisturbed, for 15 minutes. Check it after 10 minutes – if all the liquid has gone, good. If not, don't worry, just make sure the heat is good and low and let it steam, covered, for another 5 minutes.

Now add the fish and the other cooked ingredients and stir them in with a fork, very gently again so that you don't smash up the rice. Add the remaining butter last and check the seasoning. Allow the ingredients to sit together over the same gentle heat for another 5 minutes then serve, garnished with the egg and parsley.

Chicken and rice fricassee. Historically speaking, a fricassee was chicken cooked in its own stock. Vegetables were added to the pot, then the results thickened with egg yolks. The dish that follows is a nursery version where the thickening is done with rice. It is one of those dishes you can taste before you have finished reading the recipe, so gloriously uncomplicated is the flavour. We have all been here.

You can poach a whole hen and pick it if you like, but I'm going to prescribe effortlessness instead because I'm sure that if you're in the mood for this kind of thing you might want to produce it quickly. Buy free-range chicken breasts 'supremed' (chef speak for skinless and boneless).

For 4 people you need:

150g/5oz (raw weight) long- or short-grain rice

2 tbsp butter

1 large onion, chopped

1 large carrot, sliced into rounds

1 stick celery, chopped

1 level tsp salt

4 chicken breasts, skinned, boned and cut into fairly large dice

600ml water. If you have it handy add ½ tsp court bouillon powder

50g/2oz frozen peas, thawed

50g/2oz frozen sweet corn, thawed

1 tbsp plain flour

Put the rice in a pan with 200ml/7fl oz of water, cover the pan and cook gently until the rice is soft and the water has all gone. It will take between 10–15 minutes. As soon as it is cooked, spread the rice on a baking tray or similar surface to stop it cooking any more.

Heat 1 tablespoon of the butter in a wide-bottomed saucepan and gently fry the onion, carrot and celery for 1 or 2 minutes. Add the salt, stir once more, cover the pan and really lower the heat. Let the vegetables sweat gently for about 10 minutes, then add the chicken pieces with 300ml/½ pint of water. Cover, bring to a simmer and cook for another 10 minutes or until the chicken is cooked through. Add the peas and sweet corn and simmer for another 5 minutes.

Now strain the chicken and vegetables through a colander, catching all the liquid in another pan or bowl. Keep both to hand. Return the pan to the heat and add the rest of the butter. As soon as it is bubbling, add the flour and stir together. Cook the paste gently for a minute or so, then slowly add some of the liquid from the chicken and vegetables. Keep adding until you have as much of this very light sauce as you want, then, when it has thickened, add the chicken, vegetables and rice. Let it all heat through so it is piping hot, check the seasoning (remember that it won't knock your block off with its 'intense' flavour!) and serve immediately.

Risi e bisi. I made the conscious decision to include only one risotto in this book. Although for me risotto is the first dish I would turn to for comfort, it is a complex subject that I could bang on and on about for hours. What's more, no matter how reassuring a cook tries to be about guiding the reader through risotto lore, the sheer volume of information and attention to detail that one ends up imparting can make it seem like an intimidating subject

So, here is the easiest, peasiest (sorry!) risotto you could wish for. It is entirely suited to this book because it is beloved by adults and children alike. Although on the surface of it the cooking method is like the one followed to make risotto, all the rules are out of the window when it comes to achieving that perfect chewy, creamy texture. Which means, in short, that you can't balls it up because it can be as sloppy or soupy as you like. In fact, it isn't, strictly speaking, a risotto at all. In Venice, where it comes from, it is sometimes described as a soup. I am sure a group of foodies could argue about what it is or isn't for hours, but I think you should regard it as risi e bisi, something in a league of its own.

A word about the stock: if you have chicken stock around, good for you. Since I always make this on a whim and since it is a dish of the most childlike simplicity I nearly always end up using water from the kettle and resorting to a level teaspoon of my itinerant stock powder, which is Marigold's court bouillon.

For 4 people you need:

2 tbsp olive oil

2 medium onions, very finely chopped

3 or 4 sage leaves, chopped

100g/3½oz unsmoked pancetta or bacon, chopped

150g/5oz risotto rice

½ tsp tomato purée

2 litres/3½ pints simmering vegetable or chicken stock (see above)

250g/8oz frozen petis pois or garden peas, thawed

salt to taste

1 generous tbsp unsalted butter

50g/2oz freshly grated Parmesan cheese

Heat the olive oil gently in a wide-bottomed saucepan, the bigger the pan the better.

Add the onions and sage and fry them very gently until they are softened. Do not let them brown. Add the bacon and stir it in thoroughly.

Add the rice and tomato purée and stir them thoroughly. Now start to add the stock. Pour on enough to cover the rice by about 2cm/½in. Allow it to cook, stirring often (but not slavishly), at a point that is barely simmering, until all the liquid is absorbed.

Now add roughly the same amount of liquid again, plus the peas. By the time this lot of stock has gone I almost guarantee that the rice will be spot on. If it isn't, just add a little more liquid, say one ladleful. It doesn't matter now if the rice is a little wet when it is done. That is what you want. Check the seasoning (add as much salt as you want) and fold in the butter with half the cheese. Serve the rest at the table with the risotto.

Variations. You can make this without the bacon, in which case it becomes 'risi e piselli'. I love to make it with plenty of fresh mint or basil thrown in at the end. If you eat fish, but not meat, substitute prawns for the bacon, but omit the Parmesan. Italians would never dream of adding cheese to a fishy risotto!

Fried rice. No one in south-east Asia would even think about throwing out leftover rice, and this is the Oriental equivalent of bubble and squeak. What gets thrown into the pan with the rice really depends on what is knocking around from household to household.

Successful fried rice is really about the seasoning and the order in which you cook the ingredients. The rice should always come last and wrap itself around the other ingredients. It needs to be pretty dry so that it can absorb the seasoning and not go sticky, which is why leftover rice is ideal.

How to contrive rice leftovers. Just-cooked rice does not behave the same way as leftovers. The rice is too delicate and soft to fry and it will go very sticky if more heat is applied. You can get round this by following the instructions for cooking rice on page 116 and spreading it immediately onto a small baking tray. You should chill the rice for as long as you keep it.

Here then is the basis for good fried rice. It is based on my favourite version, the Indonesian nasi goreng, which is slightly spicy. Omit the chilli by all means if you don't fancy it. The most common way to add extra nourishment to this dish is to use egg. Meat is sometimes thrown in, too, but we will deal with that later. Don't be too surprised at the addition of tomato ketchup. Our familiar version comes from a south-east Asian recipe ('Kecap' is the Malay word for sauce).

For 4 people you need:

3 tbsp vegetable or ground nut oil

2 eggs, beaten

1 small chilli, seeded and finely chopped

1 medium onion, chopped, or 4 to 5 spring onions, sliced

2 level tbsp soy sauce

½ tsp sugar

1 level tsp tomato ketchup

400g/ oz cooked, cold, long-grain rice

Heat a wok fiercely with 1 tablespoon of the oil. Pour in the eggs and allow them to cook like an omelette. Just as the egg is setting, break it up with the end of a wooden spoon and when it looks good and dry remove it from the wok.

Heat the remaining oil and add the chilli, then the onions. Stir-fry them briskly for a couple of minutes, then add the rice, plus all the seasonings. Return the eggs to the fray and stir-fry everything together for a couple more minutes or until the rice is heated through.

Optional additions include:

Meat: Cooked ham or finely diced bacon works best. Cook it before the eggs and remove it from the wok before you make the omelette. Return the meat to the wok with the rice.

Vegetables: Anything you like really, although shredded cabbage, tofu, peas, very finely chopped broccoli or peppers are best. Fry them with the onions and chilli.

Fish or seafood: Prawns being the most obvious choice. Fry them hard in the wok until fully cooked, again before you do anything else. Return them with the rice.

Two rice puddings.

For better or worse, most people now associate rice pudding with a quick, tinned dessert. 'Creamed rice' from a tin can be delicious. However, it is not really a rice pudding, which should be delicately spiced and baked. It must have a skin on the top. You need a good 3 hours to make the traditional rice pudding. The oven needs to be on a very low setting.

For 4 people you need:

50g/2oz round pudding rice

1 litre/1¾ pints full fat milk (look for the extra rich 'breakfast milk', made from Guernsey cows that you sometimes see in the shops)

50g/2oz caster sugar

25g/1oz butter

¼ nutmeg

Preheat the oven to 140°C/275°F/mark 1.

Combine the rice with half the milk and all the sugar in a pie dish and bake for 1 hour.

Remove the rice from the oven and stir in the butter with the rest of the milk and bake for another hour

Remove from the oven and stir again. This time grate the nutmeg onto the surface of the pudding before cooking for 1 final hour.

Serve the rice pudding with jam, marmalade and/or single cream if you wish.

Cheating.

I developed this cheat's rice pudding over the years for three reasons. The first is the time (this method halves the cooking time), but the second is the fact that I don't keep a store of pudding rice. I do have risotto and basmati in more often than not and both will make a fine 'rice pud'. Basmati actually makes a very fragrant dessert so I don't spice it at all. The spicing of rice puddings is the third reason for the following version. Over time I've noticed that lots of people don't really like 'nutmeggy' puddings. So this one is flavoured with vanilla, in the French style. Once more, do omit the vanilla if using basmati so that you catch its unique but delicate flavour. If you must spice a basmati pudding try one or two pods of cardamom, just crushed and thrown in.

For 4 people you need:

100g/3½oz risotto rice

50g/2oz caster sugar

200ml/7fl oz milk

1 drop vanilla essence or the seeds from ¼ vanilla pod

100ml/3½fl oz single cream

25g/1oz butter

Preheat the oven to 150°C/300°F/gas 2.

Put the rice in a small pan with 200ml/7fl oz of water and heat gently. Don't stir it at all, just let the water disappear. It will take about 15 minutes.

Combine the cooked rice, sugar, milk, vanilla essence or seeds and cream in a pie dish. Bake for 1 hour then remove from the oven. You will already have the start of a skin. Blob the butter onto the surface of the pudding and return it to the oven for a further 30 minutes. Serve when the skin is golden and wrinkly.

Cold rice pudding makes a marvellous dessert with poached pears (see page 162) and a sprinkling of flaked almonds.

A bar of chocolate. The 21st century must be a confusing time for the self-confessed chocoholic. Until fairly recently it was a vice right up there with cigarettes and alcohol, but lately it is enjoying a very public rehabilitation as something of a virtue. It has long been recognized as the best cure in the world for a broken heart, but recently much has been made of cocoa's polyphenol content. In layman's terms this is a substance (also found in greens like spinach and broccoli) known to combat ageing and disease. Today's nutritionists are really only echoing the beliefs of our medical forefathers who promoted chocolate as a 'cure all' when it first made its way to Europe in the seventeenth century.

I've had a hard time working chocolate into this book. There is no shortage of things to say about its value as a comfort food. The difficulty presented itself in trying to decide what recipes to include and where to start!

When we want soup to warm our cockles we might take time out to make it. When we want mash to rejuvenate us we can sum up the patience to boil potatoes. When the craving for chocolate strikes the most obvious thing to do is to raid the local newsagents' for whatever bar of confection seems most enticing at that moment. Sadly, those sweet and chewy mouthfuls of pleasure are a world away from the dark and bitter stuff that is supposed to enhance your mood and zap a few free radicals in the process. The most you will get from your average choccie bar is a sugar rush.

How do we get round this problem? My answer is to try and keep a stock of *real* cooking chocolate lurking in the fridge. I must admit that I don't always manage to keep it for cooking. I'm a terrible fridge raider. Incidentally, by cooking chocolate I mean something that is made up of at least 70% cocoa solids and not the nasty, tasteless kind sometimes sold under the same name. I think we buy so many commercially made bars of chocolate as adults because we have an abiding memory of how bad some of that stuff used to be. You need to read the packaging and look for the magic percentage. There is any number of great brands around, but my favourite is currently Green and Blacks, who sell a cooking chocolate with a heart-pounding 72% cocoa. This is not to be recommended as a midnight feast. You might as well make yourself a double espresso and wait for the dawn before you will be able to sleep. They also produce a great cocoa powder and, lately, a number of milk chocolate-type bars with a deeper, darker taste than many of their rivals

A classic chocolate mousse.

I love dark, barely sweet chocolate mousse, especially served with fresh raspberries which go well with chocolate but also counteract the richness. This is incredibly quick to make, but is another of those things that people tend to buy in, thus cheating themselves of real luxury. You could put the mousse into small pots or ramekins or make it in a large bowl and serve it by the spoonful.

For 4 portions you need:

- 200g/7oz bitter chocolate
- 4 eggs, separated
- 1 tbsp or 30g/1½oz of unsalted butter
- 2 tbsp strong coffee
- 1 tbsp vodka

If you are not serving the mousse with raspberries, any liqueur, or brandy will do in place of the vodka

Melt the chocolate and butter together in a bowl over hot water. While still warm, beat the egg yolks in one by one. The mixture will go glossy.

Now beat the egg whites in a large bowl until they form stiff peaks. Add the vodka and a spoonful of the egg whites to the chocolate to loosen the mixture up. Carefully fold in the rest of the whites. Pour into a serving bowl or ramekins and chill for at least 2 hours before serving.

A very simple chocolate tart.

I just couldn't resist including this recipe from the cookbook *Roast Chicken and Other Stories* by Simon Hopkinson and Lindsey Bareham. It is an intensely chocolaty tart that, once you have sorted out the pastry, takes no time to prepare and cook.

For a 20.5cm/8in tart case you need:

250g/9oz sweet short crust pastry

3 egg yolks

2 whole eggs

2 tbsp (roughly 30g/1½oz) caster sugar

150g/5oz unsalted butter

200g/7oz bitter chocolate, broken into pieces

Roll out the pastry into a disc large enough to line the base and sides of your tart case. Press the pastry into the case and trim off any excess round the edges, then prick it all over with a fork. Now put the case in the fridge to chill for about 30 minutes.

Preheat the oven to 220°C/425°F/mark 7 and place a tray large enough to hold the pastry case inside.

When both tray and oven are hot, bake the pastry case for about 15 minutes, or until golden brown. Remove and allow to cool slightly.

Turn the oven down to 190°C/375°F/mark 5

Beat the eggs and sugar until they are pale and fluffy, and then set them to one side.

Gently heat the butter and when it has melted, add the chocolate. When the chocolate has melted, pour the mixture over the eggs. Beat the two mixtures together and pour them into the pastry case. Return the tart to the oven for just 5 minutes. It will continue to set as it cools.

I mentioned above that the chocolate mousse is good with raspberries and so is this. You can scatter them into the chocolate filling just as you are about to put the tart in the oven, since the cooking time is so brief. They will only just get the chance to bleed a little and the effect is very satisfying. Alternatively you can just serve them on the side.

Chocolate mousse cake.

Sometimes you see this referred to as chocolate soufflé cake, which is odd, since it is designed to collapse. It is essentially a baked mousse, and because it contains no flour it packs a hugely chocolaty punch. The collapsing of the cake actually works to your advantage because you can enjoy it two ways. Soon after making it you can serve it barely cooked – it manages to be fluffy and gooey all at once. Later on (and particularly the next day) it becomes very, very dense. I like it best that way and often make it a day ahead of dishing it up.

If like me you're not keen on coffee in cakes, rest assured that its inclusion here is working on a very subliminal level. It enhances the bitter chocolate rather than flavouring the cake.

For a 20.5cm/8in cake tin you need:

200g/7oz bitter chocolate, broken into pieces

100g/3½oz unsalted butter

6 eggs, separated

2 tbsp of black coffee (instant is fine)

3 level tbsp of icing sugar

Grease the cake tin and line it with parchment. Preheat the oven to 200°C/400°F/mark 6.

Gently heat the butter in a pan over a low heat and when it has melted, fold in the chocolate. When that has melted too, set it to one side.

Beat the egg yolks with 2 tablepoons of the sugar until pale and fluffy. Fold in the chocolate and butter, then fold in the coffee and set aside.

Beat the egg whites with the remaining caster sugar until they form soft peaks. Whisk about a third into the chocolate mix to loosen it and then carefully fold in the rest, keeping it as bubbly as possible. Transfer to the cake tin and bake for 30 minutes. Whatever you do don't open the oven door during this time because the cake might collapse too early. After 30 minutes remove the cake. Don't worry if it seems very wobbly, that is part of its charm. It will still cook as it cools. Allow the cake to rest for a good hour before eating if you plan to use it that day. Otherwise store in a cool place (not the fridge) overnight.

Chocolate praline cake.

The praline refers to the broken up, roasted nuts which replace flour as the bulk of this cake. It is a little like a grown-up brownie. You could use any nuts you like really, but hazelnuts or almonds are best. Again this is very easy to make. I particularly like the way that all the weights are the same. It also keeps well, so you can make it a day or so in advance.

For a 20.5cm/8in cake tin you need:

200g/7oz roasted hazelnuts, without skins

200g/7oz bitter chocolate, broken into pieces

200g/7oz unsalted butter, very soft

200g/7oz caster sugar

4 eggs, separated

Grease and line the cake tin with parchment. Preheat the oven to 150°C/300°F/mark 2.

Roughly grind the hazelnuts and the chocolate pieces. You want gravel rather than a powder, if that makes sense. Transfer them to a bowl and set aside.

In a separate bowl, beat the butter and sugar together until pale and fluffy, then add the egg yolks one by one. Fold this mixture into the chocolate and nuts and set aside.

Beat the egg whites until they form soft peaks. Whisk about a third of the whites into the nut mixture to loosen it and then carefully fold in the rest. You want to keep the mixture as bubbly as possible.

Bake for 45 minutes or so before checking the cake. Insert a skewer or a small knife into the centre If it comes out clean the cake is ready.

Allow it to cool completely before turning out.

A cup of cocoa. **It may seem strange to include a recipe for something as obvious as hot chocolate in a recipe book. Sadly few of us get to experience the real joy of a cup of cocoa these days. Sweet or malted 'whatever' in hot milk is a delicious, but altogether different drink. Sachets that claim to give you hot chocolate straight from a kettle with no fat or fuss (or fun) are just horrible. A treat is a treat and for this one to work its real magic you need to set aside 5 (rather than 2) minutes of a wintry evening. If that sounds too labour intensive I must warn you that there will also be a milk pan to wash up as well as the mug afterwards. The horror!**

Real hot chocolate is best made with cocoa powder. Add your own sugar as you would to tea or coffee, in the mug. You may find that you develop a taste for the slightly bitter, truly unsweetened way the French tend to drink it.

For one large mug you need:

approx. 200ml/7fl oz milk

1 level tbsp cocoa powder

In a small saucepan, heat about a third of the milk until it is hot to the touch. Add the cocoa powder and whisk in thoroughly. Let the milk and the cocoa come to boiling point and then reduce to a simmer, stirring constantly. For a truly silky drink you need to cook out the powdery nature of the cocoa, just as you would the flour in a white sauce. It only takes 3–4 minutes. Now add the rest of the milk and bring it to scalding point. Give another gentle whisk and serve.

Caribbean ice. **This is coconut ice without the scary pink food colouring, topped with chocolate. I made it one Christmas because there never seemed to be enough of those coconut Quality Streets around. Why are they always the first to disappear? The cherries were added as a nod to a chocolate bar that made a brief, glorious appearance in the early eighties. It was obviously no rival to the Bounty bar, since it vanished without trace a few years later. It had a vaguely Caribbean sounding name. Bounty fans should note that coconut ice doesn't really resemble the filling in the chocolate bar. It's much crunchier. The glacé cherries are entirely optional.**

For a 20.5cm/8in baking tray you need:

oil for greasing

150g/5oz caster sugar

100ml/3½ fl oz milk

50g/2oz glacé cherries, roughly chopped

50g/2oz desiccated coconut

200g/7oz bitter chocolate, broken up

2 tbsp rum

Grease the baking tray and line it with parchment. Heat the sugar and milk gently in a pan big enough to hold all the ingredients. Once the sugar has completely dissolved, raise the heat and simmer for about 5 minutes.

Remove it from the heat. Combine the cherries and coconut and add them to the milk. Beat until the mixture is thick, then press the coconut ice into the tray and allow it to chill for 30 minutes.

Melt the chocolate with the rum and, as soon as it is liquid enough, pour it onto the coconut ice. Chill until the chocolate has set, then cut into cubes. This is best kept in the fridge until you want to eat it.

Mrs Went's squares. **These are chocolate and peppermint squares, in three layers. They are gloriously silly. If you are at all spooked by the notion of green colouring leave it out.**

For a 20.5cm/8in baking tray you need:

The base:

125g/4oz soft butter, plus extra for greasing

1 level tbsp cocoa powder

125g/4oz self-raising flour

25g/1oz crushed cornflakes

50g/2oz soft brown sugar

First topping:

125g/4oz icing sugar

1 tbsp peppermint essence

2 drops green food colouring

Second topping:

200g/7oz bitter chocolate

Preheat the oven to 180°C/350°F/gas 4. Grease the baking tray and line it with parchment.

To make the base, melt the butter in a pan large enough to hold all the dry ingredients. Fold these into the melted butter and mix until you have a fairly sloppy looking dough. Press this into the baking tray and pop it in the oven for 20 minutes. Allow it to cool completely before proceeding.

Mix the icing sugar, peppermint essence and food colouring with 2 tablespoons of cold water. Spread the paste over the biscuit base and chill until the icing has set.

To make the second topping, melt the chocolate with 2 tablespoons of water and cover the icing. When the chocolate has set you can cut the contents of the tray into squares.

Chocolate biscuit cake.

(Illustrated) When I was young this was sometimes referred to as fridge cake and was made with digestives. Almond essence was thrown in, so lately I have replaced the biscuits with the Italian Amaretti. These are widely available. They are like miniature, crunchy macaroons. You could really use whatever biscuit you like.

For a 20.5cm/8in baking tray you need:

- 50g/2oz butter, plus extra for greasing
- 1 tbsp caster sugar
- 2 tbsp cocoa powder
- 1 level tbsp golden syrup
- 250g/9oz roughly broken (not crumbed) Amaretti biscuits

Grease the baking tray and line it with baking parchment. Gently heat the butter, sugar, cocoa and syrup in a pan large enough to take all the ingredients. Fold in the biscuits and stir over the heat for about 1 minute.

Press the cake mixture firmly into the tray. It might be quite hot so use the end of a wooden spoon and not your fingers. Chill for 2 hours before breaking it into slices. This is best kept in the fridge so that it won't be too messy to eat with your hands.

Brownies.

A good brownie is slightly gooey in the middle and crunchy on the top. The brownie came from America, where they have a slightly sweeter tooth than ours so using a really dark chocolate makes them less sickly. The original recipe for this calls for pecan nuts, but I love it with walnuts just the same.

For a 20.5cm/8in baking tray you need:

- 125g/4oz unsalted butter, plus extra for greasing
- 50g/2oz bitter chocolate, broken up
- 50g/2oz self-raising flour
- a pinch of salt
- 125g/4oz caster sugar
- 125g/4oz broken walnut pieces
- 2 large eggs, beaten
- a drop of vanilla essence

Preheat the oven to 180°C/350°F/gas 4. Grease the baking tray and line with parchment.

Gently melt the butter and stir in the chocolate. Remove from the heat and let the chocolate melt in the warmth of the butter.

Meanwhile, sift the flour and salt into a bowl and stir in the sugar and walnuts. When the chocolate has melted pour into the flour mixture and stir to incorporate. Then, fold in the eggs and the vanilla. Pour the whole lot into the baking tray and cook for no more than 30 minutes.

The brownies may feel very soft in the middle, but the cooking continues a little as they cool. Let the mixture cool in the tray until it looks like it is shrinking away from the sides a little. Then you can cut it into squares and continue cooling on a wire rack.

A bunch of bananas. In all my years I have only met one person who could not stand bananas. I remember feeling so sorry for him because at the time we were on a bumpy journey across the lesser Sundas of Indonesia and, for me, they were the best takeaway breakfast you could ever want. I sought them out hungrily at dusty bus stands, sold on the branch.

Although the banana is a tropical fruit it has been eaten here since the 17th century, and shipped here in bulk since 1882. The beginnings of the banana trade were shaky. If ships were delayed the fruit could rot in the hold. Once advances in technology meant that the containers were refrigerated, business became brisk. Today, the banana could almost be described as our national fruit. Polls have revealed that it is more popular than the apple. The only items that outsell bananas in our supermarkets are petrol and lottery tickets.

Why do we love them so much? They are easy food, even baby food. They are definitely comfort food. One friend, trying to put his finger on the reason for their popularity, says that it is because they 'always taste like a dessert, even if they are not one'. I think this sums it up. They are sweet, rich, filling and creamy. Not many foods can be described that way without carrying a health warning. Bananas come with just the opposite. They are good for you. That said, this chapter is going to deal mainly with the wonderful puddings that they can enrich.

Most shops sell the larger, yellow, Caribbean type of banana. If you come across a rarity (and it is possible), especially the little red kind or the fat stubby Asian types, snap some up and eat them just to see how varied this fruit can be.

Bananas are one of the few fruits that can successfully ripen at home. You don't need to be too fussy about their colour when they are in the shop, since over a matter of days green bananas will turn yellow, then develop brown flecks. At which point they are perfect for eating. Then they turn browner and browner until their flesh is almost amber and highly perfumed. Lots of people don't like them this way, but that is when they shine in something like banana bread (see page 150).

The ultimate milkshake. This is a milkshake in the American style, or what Australians might call a smoothie. Before the arrival of McDonalds, Burger King and the like on our shores, shakes were just flavoured milk. No fun at all! This recipe doesn't hark back to those days. I believe that we have adopted the thick shake and the smoothie because people love creamy, slightly gloopy drinks the world over. Think of the yoghurt lassi from India, the Spanish hot chocolate or the drinks made with ripe avocadoes in Latin America. Talking of lassi, I include yoghurt in this shake. I think I originally added it to be 'healthy', but it also cuts through the sweetness of bananas. A blender, or the top attachment of a Kenwood mixer, is best for this kind of shake, but a food processor will do the trick. They tend to froth the milk a little which some people like.

The following amounts just about fill a 600ml/1 pint glass. Plenty for you to share (or guzzle alone... like I do). If making more, it is best to do it in batches as a full blender can be a scary thing when you switch it on.

To fill a 600ml/1 pint glass you need:

2 ripe bananas

1 tsp honey (optional)

1 scoop chocolate ice cream

2 tbsp natural yoghurt

200ml/7fl oz milk (skimmed is fine if that's your thing)

I find that it is easiest to blend the bananas, honey (if using), ice cream and yoghurt before adding the milk. Make sure the lid is on tightly so that you don't get splashed. Add the milk when you have a smooth pulp. If it seems too thick, by all means add more milk than I've prescribed.

A fruitier, sharper version can make a great start to the day. Here is my breakfast version.

The breakfast version:

2 ripe bananas and a handful of soft fruit (strawberries, mango or raspberries are ideal)

3 tbsp natural yoghurt

100ml/3½fl oz apple juice

1 tsp honey

400ml/14fl oz milk

Again, blend the bananas, fruit and yoghurt before adding the milk, honey and apple juice.

Stuffed bananas. **(Illustrated) A pud for people who profess to hate making dessert. This is so easy! It calls for ripe bananas and chocolate buttons. We all know the famous make of chocolate buttons and they do the trick very nicely, but if you are feeling adventurous or sophisticated (I use these terms very loosely!) try white chocolate buttons. There are also dark chocolate buttons around if you care to look them up: they are sometimes rather coyly marketed as 'pistoules' of chocolate. Don't even think of trying to foist those on children. Stick with you-know-who's to avoid disappointment and recriminations.**

This is the perfect way to round off a barbecue, since you can cook it on the coals after all the savoury foods. If you plan to do this, have the bananas ready-stuffed and wrapped, so that you can slap them straight over the fire once you are done with the main course. I won't give you a cooking time for barbecues; that really depends on how hot yours is. Neither does it really matter how squishy the banana is inside, there is plenty of tastebud-thrilling going on with the chocolate.

Slit 1 unpeeled banana per person (this is surprisingly rich stuff) down the length, stopping just shy of each end so that they are not cut in half. Gently squidge the banana to allow you to stuff about 6 chocolate buttons into each slit. Wrap tightly in foil and, if cooking in a conventional oven, give them 30 minutes at 180°C/350°F/gas 4. Be careful when you open them as the flesh will be very hot. If you are serving them to children, it's best to open theirs for them.

Banana custard. **I like to roast bananas before letting them go cold, then adding them to the finished custard. You do not need to do this, but it does add a slightly caramelized taste to the finished dessert. If you are screwing up your nose at this because you suffered at the hands of school banana custard, I can only reassure you, as I have elsewhere in this book, that this is totally different.**

Allow 1 banana per person so that this is banana custard (not custard with bananas). Roast them, wrapped tightly in foil, for 20 minutes at 160°C/325°F/gas 3 and allow to cool before handling them. They should be slightly toffeeish and yet firm enough to roughly slice into the custard. For children follow the basic custard recipe on page 172. If serving adults (and why not?) make the spiced custard recipe on page 179, and just before serving lace it with a tiny splash of rum or Kahlua.

The ultimate banana sandwich.

These are a great way to use bananas that are on their last legs. I will actually go further than that and say that this will not work with anything other than a really ripe nana.

The bread should be brown, but white will do. It must be cut thick and is easiest eaten with the crust removed. For me, in all my gluttony, it should also be spread with a generous amount of butter, but I know of those who recommend cream cheese or peanut butter instead. Both alternatives are delicious.

For each sandwich you need:

1 very ripe banana
1 tbsp milk
1 tsp honey or caster sugar
2 slices brown bread

Lightly mash the banana, milk and honey or sugar together (don't blend them in a food processor because they will liquefy). Spread on the bread just before serving. Banana sandwiches can go soggy so it's better not to make them in advance.

This may seem a little wacky but do try, just once, adding a tiny pinch of freshly ground black pepper to the filling. There is a long tradition of adding a lacing of heat to sweet dishes in some parts of the world. I know of people who prescribe it for Christmas cake, for instance. You will not taste the pepper in a conscious way, but it will intensify the sweet kick of the banana. An alternative is nutmeg, but you must be very careful not to overpower the other ingredients. Make it the tiniest pinch.

If you still own a toasted sandwich maker, like most people seemed to in the early eighties, try the above that way. Heavenly.

Butterscotch and banana mousse. **As a famous advert once claimed, there are certain foods you never grow out of. Then again there are others that you feel you ought to grow out of. I have nothing but the fondest memories of various fast-setting, moussey things from my youth that went under names like Angel Delight and Instant Whip, but the spoilsport adult in me thinks of them as intrinsically 'kiddish' desserts. That is how I came up with this recipe. It was an attempt to recreate a 'school night' pudding of my mother's, which involved throwing chopped banana into butterscotch-flavoured Angel Delight. The results were fantastic, a sort of precursor to the Banoffee Pie. It follows that if you are less of a glutton for punishment than me you can knock up the original in about 5 minutes flat. Or you can try the version below, make more mess and yet somehow feel like a real grown-up.**

For 4 people you need:
200g/7oz caster sugar
50ml/2fl oz double cream
1 tsp butter
6 eggs, separated
a pinch of salt
½ lemon
2 medium bananas

The first thing to do is 'ape' the butterscotch by heating the sugar in a pan with 1 tablespoon of water until it turns into caramel. This can take anything up to about 20 minutes. Take the caramel to a fairly pale stage – think of the colour of golden syrup (you could use syrup, but it has a fairly distinctive taste of its own).

Allow the caramel to cool a little, then gently fold in the cream and butter. Whisk in the egg yolks, one by one. Add the salt.

Now prepare the bowl for the egg whites by running the lemon gently around the inside. This not only helps the whites beat faster, it will add the very subtle hint of lemon that true butterscotch contains. Beat the egg whites until they form soft peaks, and fold them with the butterscotch mix.

Place the chopped bananas in a bowl and cover them with the butterscotch mousse. Allow it to set for at least 2 hours before eating.

Banana bread.

I imagine this rich loaf must have made its way here from the Caribbean, but it has become a well loved part of Britain's repertoire of tea breads. It is a cake more than anything else. The recipe I grew up with contained dried fruit and mixed nuts, but some years ago I switched to apple and walnuts. I believe they enhance, rather than dominate, the taste and texture of the bananas within. As with a banana sandwich, you should make this only with obscenely ripe bananas, so that it works very well if you find some in a fruit bowl that appear, to the untrained eye, to be 'past it'.

As well as a tea time loaf this can make a rich and not inelegant pudding. Serve warm slices next to vanilla ice cream and you will see what I mean.

For a 450g/1lb loaf tin you need:

125g/4oz softened butter (I think salted is best here, but it doesn't matter terribly), plus extra for greasing

500g/1lb 2oz ripe bananas (unpeeled weight and there is no need to be too scientific here: it's about 3 average-sized fruits)

grated flesh of 1 eating apple (approx. 100g/3½oz)

1 tbsp honey or golden syrup

2 tbsp rum (optional)

250g/9oz self-raising flour

1 tsp mixed spice

125g/4oz golden caster sugar

125g/4oz walnut pieces, chopped

2 eggs

Preheat the oven to 150°C/300°F/gas 3. Grease the loaf tin (there is no need to line most modern ones).

Mash the peeled bananas with the butter. Add the apple, honey and rum (if using).

Sift together the flour and mixed spice, then mix in the sugar and walnuts and stir into the banana mix. Finally, add the eggs, one by one, and stir vigorously. A mixer with a cake paddle is perfect for this job. Don't use a food processor as you will end up with a smooth batter.

Pour the cake mixture into the tin and bake for 1½ hours before checking. If a fork or skewer does not come out clean in the middle, return the tin to the oven and check again every 10 minutes or so.

When the loaf is ready, rest it in the tin for at least 5 minutes before turning out onto a cooling rack. Like the banana sandwich (see page 148), this is delicious spread with cream cheese. Another, more surprising, spread for banana loaf is raspberry jam, although that is for real sweet toothers only.

Banoffee pie. Banana and toffee: ban–offee. What the *Daily Telegraph* once, rather sneeringly, called 'the staple of middle-class dinner parties'. To be fair to that journalist, there was a time when banoffee was everywhere. From the late eighties through the early nineties this pudding was downright trendy. At that time I wrongly imagined it to be a recent, American import. It has the feel of Americana about it; they have that way of utilizing bought-in ingredients like condensed milk and digestive biscuits (Graham crackers in the States). Anyway, it belongs neither to the eighties, nor the USA.

Banoffee pie was actually invented in a restaurant called the Hungry Monk, near Eastbourne, in 1971. There's a plaque outside to prove it. The owner once got a written apology from a well-known supermarket who sold it as an American pudding! And how do I know? Because it says so on the website. Oh yes, there's a banoffee website! It's devoted to the improvement and evolution of the banoffee pie.

The pie is really a sort of assembly kit. You can make it in a bowl, like a trifle. I use a Pyrex kind of dish, 20.5cm/8in across, like your average cake tin. Once upon a time banoffee pie and millionaire's shortbread (see page 76) involved boiling tins of condensed milk for hours until you achieved toffee. Seeing as this book is about comfort cooking and not extreme sports I have another method that I received from Nestlé on how to achieve this quickly and safely.

For 4–6 people you need:

50g/2oz butter

250g/9oz digestive biscuits, crushed

3 medium ripe bananas, sliced

300ml/½ pint double cream

1 tsp honey

For the toffee:

125g/4oz butter

100g/3½oz caster sugar

2 tbsp golden syrup

200g/7oz condensed milk (this is usually sold in tins of 397g so we are really talking about half a tin. Don't mess up your scales by weighing it out)

Optional extra:

chocolate shavings or coffee powder

Melt the butter and mix it into the crushed biscuits. Line the base of the bowl or tin with the biscuit base and set aside.

Follow the instructions for making condensed milk into toffee on page 76 and, when cooled slightly, pour it onto the biscuit base. Chill for at least 1 hour.

Arrange the banana slices over the toffee. Whip the cream to soft peaks with the honey and use it to top the pie. Adding the honey will not make the cream very sweet, but makes it harder to overwhip it (an old wives' tale that always seems to work).

You can serve this pie with chocolate shavings on the top. The original recipe from the Hungry Monk uses coffee powder.

Time out

Lazy Sunday. There are two fine institutions missing from this book. One is the great British fry-up. The other is roast beef and all the trimmings. I have never been much of a drill sergeant in the kitchen, which is probably why I run a pub and not the Savoy. I don't want to spend the next chapter barking orders and devising timetables.

Of course, there are people who can breeze into a kitchen and pull off a Sunday roast with the minimum of effort. Most people I know find it very stressful. They invariably do it only when they have 'people' (usually the in-laws) coming round and feel they ought to be serving up something traditional. If you ask me, this is a good enough reason not to, all by itself. In fact, visitors are the last people I would attempt a full-on Sunday roast for.

Without wanting to sound at all 'back to basics', the traditional Sunday roast is best when it is a family affair because then at least the cook has a fairly 'captive' audience. What I mean by that is one that won't get stuck in traffic. If Sunday roasts are about precision timing, the worst thing that can happen to yours is to run up against other people's.

The second worst thing to run up against is your kitchen. Mine is tiny. Give it a couple of portholes rather than no windows at all and it might just pass for a galley. Now I can produce some pretty fine meals in a small space, but roast dinner for umpteen relatives isn't one of them. There would be no point in buying a fantastic rib of beef on the bone if, having spent all that money, I had to saw it in half just to get it in the oven. And with it wedged in so tightly where would I put the potatoes, the Yorkshire pudding, the crumble I thought would be nice and the chicken for cousin thingy who gave up red meat? My cheeks have gone hot just thinking about it.

The following recipes are the kind of thing I would, and do, attempt instead. I've called them 'Lazy Sunday' because in a sense they are. For me, having people round on a Sunday shouldn't mean running around behind the scenes the whole time. I treasure Sunday as a day of rest as much as the next person. The meals that follow can pretty much be sorted out in advance of any arrivals. They have a sense of Sunday about them of course. If you are blessed with time, space and confidence you can add as much in the way of trimmings to them as you want. Roast potatoes are the obvious extra and you will find them on page 83. These meals are lighter on the plate than a traditional roast, but that's because, for me, not having room for pudding is a disaster. More on puddings will follow of course...

Stuffed breast of lamb and cauliflower cheese.

Breast of lamb is the cheapest and fattiest cut you can buy for roasting, but that is its charm. It must be slowly cooked so that it is very tender. While this happens much of the fat will melt and you see the result swimming at the base of the roasting dish. The stuffing adds an extra layer of meat because the breast is really quite a shallow cut. It also makes for a magical flavour, especially with cauliflower cheese.

For 4 people you need:

The mint sauce:

1 large bunch mint, stalk and leaves finely chopped

5 small gherkins, finely chopped

2 tbsp wine or cider vinegar

1 tbsp caster sugar

1 tsp salt

The meat:

1 tbsp olive oil

1 leek, trimmed and finely chopped

250g/9oz quality sausage meat

¼ tsp salt

1 level tsp fresh thyme

1 clove garlic, chopped

2 large boned breasts of lamb (approx. combined weight should be about 1kg/2¼lb)

The cauliflower cheese:

1 large cauliflower, cut into large florets

50g/2oz butter

25g/1oz plain flour

300ml/½ pint milk

1 tsp salt

50g/2oz Lancashire cheese

First, make the mint sauce by combining all the ingredients in a small jug. Mint sauce should be quite rough and not too liquid, but you can add more vinegar if you like. Put to one side until needed.

Preheat the oven to 220°C/425°F/gas 7. Grease a baking tray with the olive oil.

Next, deal with the lamb. Combine the leek with the sausage meat and the seasonings. Lay the lamb out flat on a chopping board, skin side down, and spread the inside with the sausage mix, stopping just shy of the edges. Roll the lamb lengthways and tie in 3 places with butcher's string. Lay the breasts in the baking tray, just slightly apart, and pour 150ml/¼ pint of water into the roasting tray. Cover with tin foil and roast the lamb for 2 hours. Remove the foil, baste the lamb with the juices and roast for a further hour.

Meanwhile, make the cauliflower cheese. Blanch the cauliflower in plenty of boiling water for about 3 minutes. Drain and set aside.

Heat the butter gently in a small saucepan and when it is bubbling add the flour. Stir together for 2 minutes until you have a paste, then add a third of the milk. Stir until the paste has dissolved into the milk, at which point it should start to thicken. Add the remaining milk and as soon as it has thickened to the point where it coats the back of the spoon add the salt and cheese. Lay the cauliflower in a suitable baking dish and pour the sauce all over it. Shake the dish gently to let the sauce settle everywhere and bake with the lamb for the last 30–40 minutes.

Salmon fishcakes.

This recipe is best with cold cooked salmon, but you could use tinned fish instead, or a poached piece of smoked haddock. If you end up with more than you need they freeze very well and can be cooked from frozen.

For 4 people (8 smallish fishcakes) you need:

200g/7oz cooked, cold, flaked salmon

200g/7oz cooked, cold, new potatoes (blitzed or thoroughly smashed up), or mash

1 heaped tbsp flour, plus extra for coating the fishcakes

1 level tsp salt

2 whole eggs and 1 egg yolk, beaten together

breadcrumbs or, even better, polenta

1 tbsp butter

1 tbsp oil

Mash the salmon and the potatoes together with the flour and salt. Add half the egg mixture and beat until well incorporated.

Flour your hands. Shape the mixture into small patties and set them aside. Now you want a sort of assembly line. Coat each cake in flour, then the remaining egg. Finally coat the cakes with the breadcrumbs or polenta.

It's a good idea to chill the fishcakes before handling them again, for at least 1 hour. Line a tray with baking parchment and pop the cakes onto the paper before putting them into the fridge. If you have to double layer them just cover the first lot with another piece of parchment. And if you plan to freeze any this is the best way to do that. If you plan to store them in a freezer long-term, you should only put them in a box or freezer bag once they are frozen. That way they will not stick together.

You can deep fry the fishcakes but I prefer to start them in a frying pan and then grill them. It is easier to cook a large batch that way, and you can use a little butter for flavour. Heat a wide-bottomed frying pan with the butter and oil. Brown each cake on both sides, then finish them under a hot grill for about 10 minutes, turning once.

Roast gammon, lentils and 'Indian coleslaw'. **Roast ham and lentils is a great combination. The coleslaw is a nickname my family gave to a Gujerati dish of very quick-cooked carrot and white cabbage with mustard seeds. It is, naturally, inspired by a Madhur Jaffrey recipe.**

Talk to your butcher about the gammon. A gammon is a leg of cured pork. Some gammon needs soaking before it can be cooked or it will be too salty. It really depends on the cure so ask the butcher. What size? I always go on about 250g/9oz per person.

For 4 people you need:

The meat:

1 joint of gammon or bacon (1kg/2¼lb will do it)

2 whole carrots

1 stick celery

2 onions, unpeeled and cut in half

3 cloves

2 bay leaves

330ml (your average bottle size) of a decent beer

olive oil

The lentils:

200g/7oz puy lentils

2 tbsp olive oil

1 tsp English mustard

a generous handful of chopped parsley

The coleslaw

2 tbsp olive oil

1 tbsp whole mustard seeds

1 whole dried red chilli (optional)

300g/11oz carrots, peeled and shredded

1 smallish white cabbage (approx. 300g/11oz), cored and finely sliced

1 tsp salt

1 tsp caster sugar

juice of 1 lemon

Preheat the oven to 220°C/425°F/gas 7.

Place the gammon in a roasting tray and surround with the vegetables, cloves and bay leaves. Add the the beer and 2 litres/3½ pints of water, then drizzle over a little oil. Cover with foil and bake for 1 hour. Then take off the foil and baste the gammon with the juices. Return to the oven and cook for 1 hour more. If you use a bigger ham then up the cooking time by 30 minutes per 500g/1lb 2oz.

Meanwhile put the lentils in a pan with plenty of water (cover them by at least 2cm/¾in). Bring them to a rapid boil and remove any scum that rises to the surface. Boil for 10 minutes (watch them fairly closely to make sure they don't bubble over), then reduce the heat and simmer until they are tender. Puy lentils can take anything from 30–45 minutes. As soon as they are tender add a ladleful of the juices from the gammon, the olive oil, mustard and parsley. Cover the pan. They will keep hot while you finish the meal.

You can enjoy the 'coleslaw' hot or cold. I love this dish cold. If you want it that way do it before everything else and allow it to cool in the serving bowl. Heat the oil in the widest-bottomed pan you have. When it is hot, throw in the mustard seeds, then cover the pan as the seeds will begin to pop. Fry for about 20 seconds then add the chilli, carrot and cabbage. Stir-fry everything for about 1 minute then add the salt and sugar. Stir-fry for another minute, then stir in the lemon juice and cook for 1 minute. Check the seasoning. It should be nice and crunchy with a sweet and sour taste. (You may be tempted to add salt but remember that the gammon is salty). Transfer to a serving bowl.

Baked salmon and horseradish sauce.

Salmon was even more of a luxury than beef when I was small. It was seasonal, wild food. Now of course we have successfully devalued it. Salmon has joined beef and poultry as the stuff of food scares and questionable ethics. Whether you worry about salmon farming's impact on the environment or not, the fish itself can be very fatty and tasteless. Nowadays I leave it alone altogether.

Wild salmon is usually available from May to September. This is the 'season', when they are caught in or near river estuaries. By this time even the smallest fish on sale will be pretty hefty, weighing in at around 2kg/4½lb. This, coupled with the price, can put you off buying a whole salmon, but it is a wonderfully easy thing to cook, and you will have fantastic leftovers for salads or fishcakes (see page 157). An alternative to a whole salmon is to buy a side or individual fillets.

At this point it is worth mentioning sea trout, which are essentially river trout that behave like salmon. They swim into river estuaries and feed on the shrimp that give the salmon that distinctive pink colour. Sea trout (sometimes known as sewyn) can be smaller and cheaper than salmon. A fishmonger should have no problem finding you one that is 1–1½kg/2¼–3¼lb in weight.

For 4 people you need:

olive oil

the salmon, either filleted or left whole, scaled and gutted (if filleted, reckon on about 250g/9oz per person)

100ml/3½fl oz white wine

2 bay leaves

2 cloves garlic

a generous pinch of sea salt

The horseradish sauce:

¼ root fresh horseradish, finely grated

½ tsp salt

½ tsp black pepper

250g/9oz double cream

juice of 1 lemon

Preheat the oven to 150°C/300°F/gas 2. Line the base of a baking tray with a piece of baking parchment and drizzle the paper with oil.

Lay the whole fish on the paper or, if using fillets, place them skin-side up. Pour the wine and 50ml/2fl oz of water around, but not over, the fish. Throw in the bay leaves and garlic and drizzle the top of the fish with more oil. Now generously scatter the salt over the fish, cover the tray with foil and put in the oven.

The fillets will cook in about 25 minutes. Cooking time for a whole salmon will depend on the size of the fish. About the smallest salmon you are likely to get, 1.5–2 kg/3¼–4½lb, will take just under 1 hour. Add another 20 minutes per additional 450g/1lb. One good way to test the fish is to tug gently at the dorsal fin. If it comes away easily the salmon is cooked through.

For the sauce, put the horseradish in a mixing bowl with the salt and pepper. Add the cream and lemon juice and beat together gently with a fork until you have the desired thickness. I like to leave mine quite loose as it will thicken up a little more while resting.

This meal is unbeatable with a new potato and green bean salad. Check out the simple potato salad on page 82 and add 100g/3½oz topped and tailed green beans per person. Or lay the just-boiled potatoes in the tray with the fish and they will eat up some of the cooking juices. Broccoli is excellent as well as the beans.

Pub chicken. **I call this pub chicken because it always reminds me of the curious fixation we had as children with 'chicken in a basket'. I have no idea who first dreamed up plonking a roast chicken into individual bread baskets, or why! This is that kind of pub-lunch-style roast. One that you want people to pick apart with their fingers. I have gone as far as serving the whole shebang on nothing more than baking parchment, which means you can gorge yourself without contemplating much washing up.**

Do yourself a favour and buy free-range, organically reared birds. My favourite chickens for roasting this way are on the smaller side. A whole poussin (spring chicken) is perfect. Giving your friends an entire bird to rip into will make for an experience that is finger licking... (no, I can't!). I cook chicken quickly, in an oven on full whack, basting it regularly in its own juices. A good guideline for time is 25 minutes per 500g/1lb 2oz.

I always serve this with glorified oven chips (see page 84), but a potato salad would do the trick.

Line a roasting tray with baking parchment and drizzle it with a little olive oil. Lay the birds breast side up on the paper and drizzle them with more oil. Sprinkle them with salt and pepper then roast them according to the guideline above. Serve the chicken on paper with plenty of kitchen towel for greasy hands. And don't hold the mayo – the recipe follows. Note that it is real mayonnaise so if you make it in advance please keep well-covered in the fridge as soon as it is done.

The mayo:

150ml/¼ pint extra virgin olive oil plus 150ml/¼ pint vegetable oil, or 300ml/½ pint light olive oil (e.g. pomace)

2 egg yolks, at room temperature

juice of ½ lemon

1 level tbsp wholegrain mustard

1 tsp salt

1 tsp black pepper

If making this by hand it's a good idea to know why you are doing what you are doing. The fat in the egg yolks and the oil are emulsifying one another. By whisking them together you are hoping that they join up. If they don't and you end up with a watery, curdled mess, it is usually for one of two reasons. One is going at it all too fast. You need to add the oil to the eggs very slowly. Ideally get someone to add it while you hold the bowl and whisk. You can watch the emulsification happening and bark 'Stop! Start!' at them to regulate the flow. Once the mayo is forming you can be more relaxed and add the oil quite steadily. When all the oil is incorporated stir in the lemon juice, mustard, salt and pepper. The other reason for split (curdled) mayonnaise is the eggs being colder than the oil, which is why they must be at room temperature. Put them into the cupboard next to the oil to be sure.

A food processor is unbeatable for the modern cook's mayonnaise. If you have one, just pop everything into it bar the oil. Start it running at full speed and add the oil in a very steady stream. Be quite bold because you need to keep up with the blades. They work faster than your hand and a whisk so adding the oil too cautiously will make the mayonnaise thicken too fast. Good mayonnaise is ready when it is thick and wobbly, almost like a jelly. Watch the blade of the machine or the whisk to see it start to cut a 'trail' through the ingredients. When it does this, you're there.

Alternative vegetable side dishes.

Braised red cabbage.

The classic accompaniment to a roast gammon, but also good with beef. Very handy for sausages and mash (see page 94). You can cook this in the oven or on the hob. Either way it should be cooked gently for about 1 hour.

For 4 people you need:

2 tbsp butter

1 medium onion, chopped

1 cooking apple, peeled, cored and chopped

1 small red cabbage (they can be enormous), you want approx 800g/1¾lb

3 tbsp wine or cider vinegar

1 tbsp brown sugar

1 tsp salt

3 cloves

a handful of dried fruit like raisins (optional)

Preheat the oven to 150°C/300°F/gas 2.

Melt the butter and gently fry the onion and apple for a couple of minutes. Add all the remaining ingredients with 100ml/3½fl oz of water and stir well to mix. Pour into a casserole dish.

Cook, covered, for a good hour or until the cabbage is dark, tender and very sweet/sour. You should keep an eye on it to make sure it isn't catching at the bottom. I often find myself adding a bit more water or another dollop of butter about halfway through the cooking time.

Leek, parsnip and mustard gratin.

This is a good alternative side dish for the lamb, gammon or salmon. It makes a fine meat-free lunch.

For 4 people you need:

6 parsnips, peeled and cut into rounds (about 1cm/½in thick)

50g/2oz soft butter

1 sprig of thyme

2 cloves garlic, roughly chopped

4 medium leeks, trimmed and thickly sliced

2 tbsp whole seed mustard

1 glass white wine

250ml/9fl oz double cream

salt and pepper to taste

First you want to leech a bit of the starch from the parsnips, as they can be claggy. Bring a pan of salted water to a boil and blanch the cut parsnips for about 8 minutes. Drain them thoroughly and set aside in an ovenproof dish.

Preheat the oven to 200°C/400°F/gas 6.

Very gently heat the butter in a wide-bottomed pan. Add the thyme and garlic and infuse for 5 minutes or so. Turn up the heat a notch and add the leeks. Shake the pan gently to cover them in the butter. Add the mustard, wine and 1 teaspoon of salt. Cover and simmer for about 10 minutes. The leeks should be softening up. Pour the contents of the pan onto the parsnips, and bake for around 15 minutes. Pour on the cream and give the dish a shake rather than stirring it in. Taste the sauce and season with salt and pepper if you wish. Bake for a further 5 minutes before serving.

Three easy casseroles. These are casseroles in the loosest use of the term, since casserole refers to the dish in which they are ideally cooked and served. A true casserole ancienne' was cooked in a mould of rice or potato and you can still find such dishes in France, where they originated. Nowadays, a casserole is generally taken to mean a heavy, ovenproof pot with its own lid. Really, only the Lancashire hot pot requires you to bake the casserole in an oven, so you could cook the other two in a large saucepan, on the hob.

Chicken in yoghurt.

I include this dish because it was a childhood favourite and because sometimes home cooking throws up an odd practice here and there. There are many stew recipes that call for the addition of canned soup. The practice is particularly popular in America. This is the best I know of. If you have made your own cream of tomato soup (see page 52) use that. If you feel odd about using a tin of soup use the equivalent amount of passata (sieved tomato).

For 4 people you need:

4 chicken crowns (or breast on the bone)

3 tbsp olive oil

2 medium onions, chopped

2 cloves garlic, chopped

1 small tin (295g) cream of tomato soup, or a similar amount of passata

250g/9oz natural yoghurt (Greek is best)

salt and pepper to taste

Fry the chicken crowns in the olive oil until nicely browned. Remove them and set aside. Add the onions and garlic to the pan with a pinch of salt, stir them and lower the heat significantly. Pop on the lid and let them sweat, covered, for about 10 minutes.

Now raise the heat and add the soup or passata. If you used tinned soup refill the empty tin with the same amount of water, and add that. When the soup has dissolved into the water add the chicken pieces and cook, covered for about 1 hour. Check the seasoning at this point.

Add the yoghurt just before serving and stir in gently. Let it simmer for just a couple of minutes so that it doesn't curdle. The ideal accompaniment to this dish, which I imagine is American, is jacket potatoes, peas and/or sweet corn.

Lancashire hot pot. **Hot pot is the most well known of the meat and potato pies that come from the north of England, and is the English equivalent of Irish stew. It takes its name from the deep, flowerpot-shaped earthenware that it was traditionally cooked and served in. The meat in a hot pot must be lamb or mutton. Originally scrag end was used and cooked on the bone, but in modern times, when economy needn't be such a consideration, most people would use neck or best end chops. I have to admit that I like mine completely off the bone, so I use diced neck or shoulder. Some recipes include one or two kidneys. While we are on the subject of the meat, I recently noticed that Betty Turpin of the famous Rovers Return makes her hot pots with beef. If anyone from Weatherfield is reading this, could they have a word?**

I use a wide casserole to make hot pot and seal my meat in that. If you are using a pie dish then you will want a frying pan to start off with.

For 4 people you need:

900g/2lb diced shoulder or neck of lamb

4 or 5 kidneys, diced (optional)

2 level tbsp flour

2 tbsp butter or dripping

2 medium onions, sliced

1 bay leaf

1 sprig of thyme

a dash of Worcestershire sauce

½ tsp salt

3 large floury potatoes, sliced

salt and black pepper to taste

Preheat the oven to 150°C/300°F/gas 2.

Toss the lamb and kidneys (if using) in the flour and season with a little salt and pepper. Heat the butter or dripping and brown the meat in small batches (so that it doesn't steam). As each batch is done, remove it to a bowl.

Now fry the onions until they are softened. Return the meat to the pot and stir everything together. Add the bay leaf and thyme, and then barely cover everything with water. You don't want it swimming. Bring the liquid to a simmer for about 15 minutes, then add the Worcestershire sauce and salt. Check the seasoning at this point. You may want more salt.

Now top the meat with the slices of potato, overlapping each slice with the next one. I season the potatoes with a pinch of black pepper. Bake the hot pot, covered for 1½ hours, then uncovered for a final 30 minutes, or until the potatoes have gone golden brown.

Beef with stout and dumplings. You could hardly dream up a more robust sounding meal. The dumplings give it the echo of a steak and kidney pudding. I thought of including steak and kidney pud here, but I think this is more of a complete meal. It is also more flexible. If dumplings don't push your buttons (or even put you off the stew) just exclude them entirely, and serve the stew over mash.

Let me reassure you, as you read the ingredients list, that this stew will not taste of chocolate. I picked up the habit of adding cocoa to stews whilst working with Spanish cooks. In Catalan cuisine it is a common practice. I now use small amounts of cocoa whenever old recipes call for gravy browning. The results are always good.

Again, this is best made in a casserole with a lid. That way, should you wish, you can bake the dumplings. They will go quite crispy and scone-like on the top, which can be lovely. Otherwise cook this like any stew, in a big saucepan on the hob.

For 4 people you need:

1kg/2¼lb stewing steak, diced
2 tbsp butter, or dripping
2 medium onions, chopped
3 medium carrots, sliced
2 bay leaves
1 level tsp salt
1 level tsp cocoa powder
1 level tbsp tomato purée
600ml/1 pint stout

The dumplings:

100g/3½oz self-raising flour
¼ tsp salt
50g/2oz shredded suet, or butter

Brown the meat in the butter or dripping, in small batches to prevent it from steaming. As it is done remove it with a slotted spoon, leaving any juices in the pot. Set aside. Soften the onions in the meat juices and return the meat to the pan. Add the carrots and bay leaves and stir together once. Add the salt, cocoa and tomato purée and stir again. Add the stout and 600ml/1pint of water, then bring everything to a simmer. Cook, covered for about 1¾ hours.

At this point check the meat for tenderness and make sure the stew is still liquid enough for dumplings. If you think it looks a little dry just add some boiling water.

If the meat is tender you can add the dumplings. Combine the flour, salt and suet (or rub in the butter as if making pastry). Add 3 tablespoons of water, 1 tablespoon at a time, and knead into a soft dough. Shape into about 16 small balls and add them to the stew. Cook, covered, for a further 20 minutes or transfer to an oven, preheated to about 200°C/400°F/gas 6 to bake the tops.

Serve immediately, with bread for mopping up the gravy.

Rare roast beef and beetroot. **I have always associated beef with extravagance. It was considered to be a luxury meat when I was younger and it still should be. Indifferent beef is not necessarily expensive, but the good stuff is. Intensive farming may have made it possible for people to eat more meat, at a lower cost, but we have paid in other ways as anyone who cares about what they eat will know. You need pasture-fed, free-range beef from a reputable butcher. Everything else is worthless.**

Rib is my favourite joint for roasting, and I always leave it pink. However, I have encountered many problems fitting a large rib, on the bone (as it should be), into a domestic oven. My own way round this has been, of late, to treat myself and my diners to the rib eye. I know this is a joint associated with steaks, but it roasts brilliantly. It is lean, but with just the right amount of fat to baste itself nicely (I never trim this off). Sirloin is slightly cheaper and is very good as well.

Preheat the oven to 250°C/475°F/gas 9.

For 4 people you need:

5 or 6 medium beetroots, with their leaves. If you can't find the leaves look for chard. You want about 600g/1lb 5oz

4 tbsp olive oil

4 tbsp wine or balsamic vinegar

1 whole rib eye (when I said this was a luxury item I meant it. The average rib eye, at 2.2kg/5lb will be expensive, but there will be plenty of meat left for eating cold. Think of the beef salad or sarnies you can make tomorrow!)

1 level tbsp unsalted butter

plenty of salt and freshly ground black pepper

Wash and trim the beetroots, reserving the greens and the stalks. Lay the roots in a roasting tray with 200ml/7fl oz of water, 3 tablespoons of the oil and all the vinegar. Sprinkle generously with salt and cover with tin foil. Place on the lower shelf of the oven and cook for 1 hour.

After the hour is up start to think about the beef. Season it by rubbing it all over with salt and pepper then heat a metal-handled frying pan or another roasting tray with the remaining oil. Brown the meat fiercely on all sides and put it in the oven.

As you put the beef in the oven remove the beetroots to see if they are tender by inserting a knife or skewer through them. If it goes through easily they are done. If not they might need another 20–30 minutes, so put them back in. When they are done, remove them from the pan, but leave the juices in the tray. Allow the beetroots to cool, then push off the skins with your fingers. Wear washing-up gloves if you are worried about your hands going a bit pink (it comes out in the wash)! Put the beetroots to one side.

Check the beef after 1 hour; it will be close to being done rare. Give it another 30 minutes or so for a more medium roast. Meanwhile, cut the beetroot into rough slices or wedges and return them to the tray with the leaves. Toss everything in the juices and stir in the butter. If the liquid seems a little scant, add a bit more water, vinegar and oil. Cover with foil again and return to the oven as you take the beef out. Rest the meat for 15 minutes while the greens cook. When the greens are done pour any juices from the joint onto them in the serving dish.

A jug of custard. Give me custard with my pudding rather than cream, any day. When I say custard, I mean the pouring kind. The French call it crème anglaise, which says everything about our love for it. Even the industrial yellow, school dinner variety seems to push some people's buttons, though I have to say I draw the line there. 'Commercially produced custard powder', wrote Jane Grigson in her book *English Food*, 'is a minor national tragedy.' She was right. True custard is not yellow and has a special, 'only just' kind of sweetness. It need not be thick with cornflour nor overpowered by vanilla essence. Even the latest wave of so-called gourmet custards can be guilty of all the above. I am no snob when it comes to buying things ready made, but I do urge you to have a go at your own custard, just once.

Baking custards as desserts is a very old practice. The ancient Greeks are meant to have mixed eggs and honey before frying them together, and the habit of baking custard may have come here with the Romans. Although custard was fairly common in Britain by the Middle Ages, its use was taken up more enthusiastically on the Continent. Here is a tale with many twists. The French may call custard 'English cream', but our modern word for the same thing is a derivative of croustade (meaning 'tart case') because baking custard in pastry was popular. In what could be described as a bizarre, cross-Channel custard pie fight, names and recipes have been flung back and forth between Britain and France for centuries. Over the years the odd dish has become better known by its French name. The most famous example of this is Cambridge burnt cream. Never heard of it? These days almost everybody calls it crème brûlée.

How to make a jug of custard.

You need:

6 egg yolks

2 tbsp caster sugar

1 tsp plain flour

600ml/1 pint whole milk (don't use skimmed, you need the fat for the custard to work)

In a bowl large enough to take the milk, beat the eggs, sugar and flour until pale and smooth.

Heat the milk gently until it looks like it is about to boil (it will 'fizz' against the side of the pan), then remove it from the heat. Whisk the milk into the egg mixture, a little at a time. You now go back to the heat to cook, and thus thicken, the custard. Select a pan that is large enough for you to suspend your mixing bowl over, fill it with water and heat to boiling point. Put the bowl on the pan and slowly and constantly stir the custard as you heat it up. The custard is ready when it starts to coat the back of the spoon. It gets thicker the longer you allow it to cook.

If you have a gas flame hob and a good, thick-bottomed saucepan you can be a little gung ho, as I tend to be, and dispense with the bowl over water. Go carefully, as custard doesn't like to be bullied. Use a very low flame – high heat under the pan will curdle the mixture and give you sweet 'scrambled eggs'. As soon as the custard has thickened, pass it through a sieve and into a cool bowl or jug and use it when you need it.

How to avoid skin on custard. It has never bothered me much, and some people love it, but if you hate the skin that forms on cooling custard, simply place a piece of clingfilm right on top of the custard, as if it were the skin itself. You lose a bit of custard as you pull off the clingfilm, but then you can't have everything.

Vanilla custard.

You will have noticed that I did not use any vanilla in my basic custard recipe. It really can dominate the flavour of something this simple and that is not always appropriate. If you would like to, infuse about a third of a vanilla pod with the milk as soon as you have warmed it up. Leave it in the milk for about 30 minutes before removing it.

Alternatively, make a vanilla sugar. This is good to have knocking around if you are the kind of person who makes puddings fairly often. You simply choose a good-sized jar and, making sure it is totally dry, drop in about 4 split vanilla pods. Fill the jar with caster sugar and leave for 2 or 3 days before using it. Once you have used most of the sugar you can refill it many times. You will know when you need to replenish the vanilla because while it is working its aromatic magic you will get a strong smell of the spice every time you open the jar. To make perfect vanilla custard, just follow the basic custard recipe above, using sugar from the jar.

Trifle. The trifles of today have been evolving since the syllabubs, custards and tipsy cakes (bread or biscuits doused in booze) from centuries gone by. The Edwardians fashioned trifle into what it should be (but sadly is not) in modern times. Trifle from a packet is a sorry affair. Nothing could be easier than the real thing, but since so many of us never make custard, few have tasted it. If you ignore my attempts to get you to make custard for any other reason, do it for a proper trifle. Everything else can be bought in and assembled quickly, without effort.

The Edwardians made trifles with jam, and somehow we have ended up using fruit jellies today. For a rich, modern trifle I use neither. I love to make mine with a mixture of whatever summer fruits I can get my hands on. Everything else in the trifle is so sweet that you get a wonderful layer of tartness if you do it my way. By all means use a jam or make a jelly like the orange one in the recipe on page 176.

Summer fruits can work out on the expensive side; I never buy them out of our growing season when their price can be prohibitive. Besides, they are not exactly bursting with flavour when air-freighted from who knows where. Several supermarkets do excellent mixtures of frozen summer berries (sometimes rather pretentiously labelled as 'forest' fruits). As they thaw they 'macerate' in their own juices (that is to say, they sort of cook without heat), which makes them perfect for the recipe below and for summer pudding (see page 200).

For 6 people you need:

The custard:

200ml/7fl oz milk

250ml/9fl oz double cream

6 egg yolks

150g/5oz caster sugar

2 tbsp cornflour

For everything else:

450g/1lb mixed berries or fruits

juice of 1 lemon

1 tbsp caster sugar

1 packet sponge fingers or a loaf of Madeira cake

1 glass of sweet sherry or dessert wine

250ml/9fl oz double cream

hundreds and thousands are optional (I hate them but it's up to you!)

First make the custard. Heat the milk and cream to scalding point (it will fizz against the side of the pan). In a separate bowl, whisk the eggs, sugar and cornflour until thick and pale. Add this mixture to the milk and cream and combine gently with a whisk. Heat the custard gently (see opposite page) until thickened. It doesn't take long because of the cornflour. Chill immediately and allow it to set – overnight is ideal.

If you are using frozen berries all you need to do is thaw them. If not, clean the fruits and remove vines, stalks etc. Then heat them for literally a couple of minutes with the lemon juice and sugar. As soon as things look a bit wilted, remove them and allow them to cool completely in their juice.

Line the bottom of a large glass bowl with a single layer of sponge fingers or broken bits of Madeira cake and douse them in sherry. This part is down to personal choice. If children are going to be eating the trifle I find that they tend to dislike too much, if any, booze. An excellent alternative is apple juice if you want to go teetotal here.

Pour the berries and all the juices onto the sponge layer – don't worry if the base looks too juicy at this point, the fingers will absorb a lot more liquid than you think. Next, spoon on the custard. Just before serving, whisk the cream to soft peaks and cover the custard with it. Decorate as you wish and serve.

Custard tart. **This is the old-fashioned, English (or French) kind of tart. You don't see it so much now, save in some traditional bakeries. I point this out because there has been a welcome invasion of late, from Portugal. The little *pasteis de nata* (sometimes known as *belem*) are suddenly everywhere. They are delicious, but they are also the work of nocturnal experts in fierce pizza style ovens. Do what everyone in Lisboa does and buy them in. A couple of the famous coffee bars now lining many of our high streets seem to have them on the menu at all times.**

This tart is easy to make. Like treacle tart, the sweetness of the filling is best served by using savoury short crust pastry.

For a 20.5cm/8in tart case you need:

250g/9oz short crust pastry

2 whole eggs

1 egg yolk

25g/1oz caster sugar

300ml/½ pint milk (not skimmed or semi skimmed, it doesn't work)

a generous pinch of grated nutmeg

Roll out the pastry into a disc large enough to line the base and sides of your tart case. Press the pastry into the case and trim off any excess round the edges, then prick it all over with a fork. Now put the case in the fridge to chill for about 30 minutes.

Preheat the oven to 220°C/425°F/mark 7 and bake the pastry shell for 10 minutes then set to one side.

Lower the heat in the oven to 150°C/300°F/mark 2.

In a mixing bowl, beat the eggs and sugar with the nutmeg until the mixture is pale and thick.

Heat the milk to scalding point in a small pan and whisk it gradually into the egg mix. Pour the mix carefully into the tart and bake again for about 30 minutes before checking to see if it has set. The filling may still be very wobbly in the middle. Give it another 5 minutes if you are not sure, but it will set further as it cools.

This is a tart best eaten cold. Like the *Crema catalana* it is lovely with fresh raspberries or, for really indulgent moments, a blob of your favourite jam.

Treacle tart. **Treacle tart has to be one of the most outrageously sweet puddings on the planet. It might also be one of the best. After years of hiding out in Gentleman's clubs and school canteens, it has crept back onto the menus of a few restaurants. Almost every single one insists on presenting it to you with a dollop of crème fraiche. No doubt 'proper' chefs think that this will do something to redeem the effects of the overwhelming sugar content on our palettes. Wrong, wrong, wrong! Somehow, as horrific this might sound to dentists everywhere, this dessert has to arrive at the table surrounded by a moat of custard.**

For a 20.5cm/8in tart case you need:

- 250g/9oz short crust pastry
- 100g/3½oz fresh breadcrumbs
- juice and zest of 1 lemon
- 1 tsp dried ginger
- 100g/3½oz treacle
- 300g/11oz golden syrup

Roll out the pastry into a disc large enough to line the base and sides of your tart case. Press the pastry into the case and trim off any excess round the edges, then prick it all over with a fork. Now put the case in the fridge to chill for about 30 minutes.

Preheat the oven to 220°C/425°F/mark 7 and bake the pastry shell for 10 minutes then set to one side.

Put the breadcrumbs in a bowl. Add the lemon, ginger, treacle and golden syrup and beat together with a spoon until everything is incorporated.

Transfer the filling into the tart case and bake again for about 30 minutes. Keep a close eye on it as the oven is hotter than for most desserts. The filling should go a fairly golden brown and look slightly 'set'. This pudding can be served hot or cold...but don't forget you know what!

Orange jelly and custard.

Okay, try and banish images of Victorian orphans singing 'food, glorious food' from your mind – this is definitely a dessert for grown-ups. The jelly is orange and lemon, razor sharp. This is so easy to make, but it looks great at the end of a dinner party, since you can serve the whole thing in outsize wine glasses rather than bowls. Jelly on the bottom, custard on top. When the two flavours meet on the tongue it is heavenly. If you can bear it, make your own orange juice (which works out a bit more expensive than buying it in). About 12 oranges will make enough juice for this recipe.

For 6 wine glasses or a medium-sized bowl you need:

The jelly:

150ml/¼ pint lemon juice

12g or 5 leaves gelatine (leaf gelatine is by far the easiest kind to use)

500ml/17fl oz unsweetened orange juice

The custard:

800ml/1¼ pints double cream

2 slices orange zest

8 egg yolks

4 tbsp caster sugar

First make the jelly. Heat the lemon juice very gently with 2 tablespoons of water, add the gelatine and leave to dissolve. Then stir it into the orange juice and pour into a bowl, jelly mould or wine glasses (I rather like the kitsch effect of the latter). Leave the jelly to set firm – the perfect excuse to make this a day ahead of serving.

To make the custard, heat the cream with the orange zest and leave to infuse for 30 minutes, then remove the zest.

Beat the eggs and sugar until pale and smooth. Combine them with the infused cream and gently reheat, stirring constantly, until thick (see page 172). This custard, when cooled, will set slightly.

When the jelly is completely firm, top with the cooled custard and chill until needed.

Once you have this dessert under your belt the variations are endless, but one that I am very fond of is to use blood oranges while they are in season. The violent colour contrast between the jelly and the custard is the main reason for this (shallow, but true!). We did the photography for this recipe in February, when the blood oranges are at their best. So hopefully you can see what I mean from the photo.

Chocolate custard and pears. **This must be a clumsy, nursery version of an old French dessert called 'poires belle Hélène' (a rather bizarre combination of poached pears, ice cream, crystallized violets and warm chocolate sauce). Poached pears are not the obvious partner for chocolate. Do try them together though because you may end up smitten. It goes without saying that you can substitute a good chocolate ice cream for the custard.**

About the pears: it is easy to poach your own and there is something very rewarding about producing home-made poached pears (for a start they look so posh). If, however, you want to use tinned pears then go ahead. Without wanting to upset true pear enthusiasts, I think they are the one fruit that 'cans' very well. The custard takes no time to make so this becomes a very quick dessert if you use the tinned fruit.

For 4 people you need:

100g/3½oz caster sugar (vanilla sugar if you have it, see page 172)

4 pears, peeled, halved and cored

juice of 1 lemon

The custard:

600ml/1 pint whole milk

6 egg yolks

1 tbsp sugar

2 tbsp cocoa powder

To poach the pears, heat the sugar with 600ml/1 pint of water until boiling, then reduce to a simmer, stirring all the time until the sugar has dissolved and the water is clear. Add the pears and the lemon juice and bring to the boil again. Boil the pears for about 1 minute, then reduce the heat to a gentle simmer, cover and cook until the pears are tender but still holding their shape. How long that takes depends on the ripeness of the pears. Keep an eye on them. It's fairly safe to say that if you cook them for 15 minutes, remove from the heat and allow to cool with the lid on the pan they will be done by the time they reach room temperature. Remove the pears from the syrup when ready to serve and make the custard.

Heat the milk to scalding point in a heavy-bottomed saucepan (it will fizz against the side of the pan). Whisk the egg yolks with the sugar and cocoa powder until smooth and glossy. Add about a third of the milk and whisk again until all the ingredients are combined. Add the remaining milk, whisk again and return to the pan. Reheat the milk on a very gentle heat, stirring constantly, until the custard begins to coat the back of the spoon. Pour the custard through a sieve into a cool bowl, then pour over the pear halves.

This chocolate custard, barely sweet at all, is also great with something as simple as vanilla ice cream or a bowlful of chopped bananas.

Baked, stuffed apples with custard. This is a timeless, English classic. It's quite Christmassey, for obvious reasons. You can leave out the stuffing of mincemeat if you don't fancy it, in which case serve it with the spiced custard below. If you are going to use the mincemeat, stick with the plain custard recipe on page 172.

I used to make this with Bramleys. They certainly have the monopoly when it comes to cooking apples, but recently my local market had an entire stall dedicated to rarer, more interesting varieties. By far the best version of this dish I have ever tasted was made with Jonagold apples. They are a cross between a cooker and an eater because they are quite large. They have a sweet, slightly perfumed flavour and it's worth enquiring after them if you have a friendly, clued up greengrocer. Otherwise, any big apple is fine. Bramleys are sharp so you could commandeer a large 'eater' instead. You'll need a baking dish small enough for the apples to fit snugly, and not rattle around.

For 4 people you need:

4 large apples, cleaned and cored, but left whole

1 moderate-sized jar of mincemeat (the weights vary but it keeps well in the fridge)

50g/2oz butter

1 tbsp caster sugar

Preheat the oven to 180°C/350°F/gas 4.

Score the skin of each apple so that they do not burst when cooking.

Fill the core cavity of each apple with mincemeat and put them into the baking dish. Dot any spare space in the dish with the butter and sprinkle the sugar over the apples.

Bake for 30 minutes, then check them for tenderness – they should be soft, but holding their shape. Don't worry if they do explode a little. It does happen and this is not the world's most elegant pud anyway.

Serve with hot custard to warm your cockles on a winter's night!

Spiced custard. This is a delicious and thicker variation of basic custard, actually better cold, and really good with chocolate puddings for some reason. Try using it as the basis for banana custard on page 146.

You will need:

2 tbsp chopped stem ginger

2 handfuls raisins

a pinch of nutmeg

a strip of orange zest

568ml double cream, warmed

3 egg yolks

2 tbsp caster sugar

The method is similar to the basic custard on page 172. Simply infuse the ginger, raisins, nutmeg and orange zest with the warmed cream for 30 minutes before whisking into the eggs and sugar. Then follow the method on page 172. Remove the orange zest before serving.

Burnt cream **(Crème brûlée).** **Despite its simplicity, burnt cream is, nowadays, a restaurant standby. And at one point it seemed that every possible deviation from the original Cambridgeshire recipe had been attempted: passion fruit brûlée, honey and cardamom ... and so on.**

We chefs love our toys, and this is the sweet that launched a thousand blow torches. Traditionally the finished custard was sprinkled with sugar and flashed under a hot grill. The blow torching of the sugar got round the absence of a suitable grill in most homes and eliminated the risk of the custard curdling under intense heat. If you don't have a grill or a blow torch there are ways of cheating. Mine, lazy as ever, is to sprinkle the top with a little muscovado sugar, which will not be quite the same, but as it dissolves it has a very burnt, caramel-like taste. Please don't rush out and buy a blow torch, by the way, this is home cooking, not DIY.

For 4 ramekins you need:

450ml/¾ pint double cream

5 egg yolks (4 would do if the eggs are large)

2 tbsp caster sugar

½ vanilla pod, scraped out, or a drop of vanilla essence

1 tbsp icing or muscovado sugar

Heat the cream to scalding point (it will fizz against the side of the pan). Meanwhile, beat the eggs and sugar with the vanilla until pale. Pour about a quarter of the cream onto the eggs and whisk thoroughly. Add the rest of the cream and whisk again.

Fill a large saucepan, big enough to suspend your mixing bowl over, two-thirds full of boiling water. Place the bowl over the water and stir constantly until the custard is thick. It can take anything from 10–20 minutes. Now, you can, like me, be a little more gung ho and do this part directly over the heat (in the saucepan) if you like. This custard, without any cornflour, is much less stable than some, and you can scramble it. However, if you are confident enough to do it you save a lot of time. It can take as little as 2 minutes on a low flame to thicken up nicely. Have a sieve, and another bowl, chilled in the fridge, ready to transfer it into quickly if things are looking scary. The sieve will catch anything near the bottom of the pan that might have started to go 'scrambly.'

Pour the thickened custard into the ramekins and chill. This is a good pudding to start the day before, and chill overnight. If you are going to cheat this with muscovado sugar add it about 1 hour before serving, since it will melt into the custard a bit.

To make this a real brûlée, you need to sprinkle the top of each chilled custard with icing sugar if you have it, since it grills fastest. Put about 1 tablespoon in a small sieve or tea strainer and tap it out over the tops of the ramekins. Place them under a hot grill. You must stand by the grill and not be distracted for a nanosecond while you grill crème brûlée. One false move and the custard will go sloppy again. Serve at your leisure. The caramel hardens and everyone enjoys breaking into the custard with their spoons.

Crema Catalana. **This is a popular Spanish version of burnt cream (or crème brûlée, see opposite page), often baked in terracotta over there. It has an entirely different feel to the English version, influenced, I'm certain, by the old Moorish presence on the Iberian peninsula. If you possess a largeish terracotta bowl, this can be very 'Costa Brava holiday'. You can also do it in ramekins.**

For a bowlful that will feed 4 to 6 people you need:

200ml/7fl oz milk

250ml/9fl oz double cream

2 strips lemon zest (just run a pairing knife or peeler gently down the side of a lemon in two places)

2 cinnamon sticks

6 egg yolks

150g/5oz caster sugar

2 tbsp cornflour

Heat the milk and cream in a heavy-bottomed pan to scalding point, then throw in the lemon zest and cinnamon. Remove from the heat and allow to infuse for 1 hour. Strain (or pick out the bits) and return to the pan.

In a separate bowl, whisk the eggs, sugar and cornflour until thick and pale. Add this to the milk and cream and combine gently with the whisk.

Heat the custard gently until thickened (see page 172). It doesn't take long because of the cornflour. Chill immediately – overnight is ideal.

You can grill crema catalana as you would a crème brûlée or cheat with muscovado sugar (see opposite page). This is a great summertime treat served with fresh raspberries.

Crème caramel.

Crème caramel was once the stuff of fairly posh dinner parties. It is one of those simple and old-fashioned puddings that somehow ends up tasting expensive, due to the dark, bitter caramel that encases the custard. Nowadays some pretty good ready-made versions are up for grabs. My only complaint about most of them is the overwhelming presence of vanilla, as is so often the case with anything 'custardy'. In the recipe below I've omitted it. Sometimes I use allspice or nutmeg in crème caramel. You add the tiniest pinch to the recipe below. If you want a hint of vanilla (and it really should just be a hint) use vanilla sugar (see page 172). I make my crème caramel in ramekins, but you can cook it in one baking dish.

For 4 or 5 ramekins, or 1 baking dish, you need:

150g/5oz caster sugar

150ml/¼ pint whole milk

300ml/½ pint double cream

¼ tsp freshly grated nutmeg, or ½ scraped vanilla pod (both optional)

4 eggs

For the caramel, dissolve 100g/3½oz of the sugar and 1 tablespoon of water in a small pan and cook, stirring constantly, until the mixture goes the colour of tea. You can go for a really bitter (and more authentic) caramel by taking it really dark. You will get an almost coffee-like smell from it. Being very careful now, and standing back a little, remove the pan from the heat and add another tablespoon of warm water. When it stops bubbling fiercely stir it in. How liquid is it? Loose enough to pour into and line the ramekins? If not, don't worry, just add another tablespoon of warm water and so on. Divide the caramel between the ramekins, or pour into the dish, and tip to coat the inside of each one.

Preheat the oven to 150°C/300°F/gas 2. Half fill a largeish baking tray with hot water and put in the oven (this is a bain-marie).

Heat the milk and cream together and add the nutmeg or vanilla (if using). When the mixture is at scalding point (it will fizz against the side of the pan), but has not boiled, whisk in the eggs and the remaining caster sugar. Pour the mixture into each ramekin, or the dish, and carefully pop them into your baking tray. They will take about 1 hour to cook, but after 45 minutes test the top of each one by touching lightly with a finger. If they feel set they are ready. Remove from the bain-marie and allow to cool fully (for at least 30 minutes) before serving.

To get them out of the ramekins and onto plates, simply hold a knife under some warm water and then run it around the edge of each ramekin. Put a small plate over the top of the ramekin and invert the whole thing. Tap the upturned base of each ramekin with the knife. The crème caramel should slide out when you lift the ramekin up. Magic!

Steamed puddings. If most of us had to conjure up a single dish that epitomized good old-fashioned stodge it might be one of the many types of steamed puddings. Once upon a time they took pride of place at the table, symbols of comfort and plenty. A visiting Frenchman in the seventeenth century was moved to exclaim: 'Blessed be he that invented pudding, for it is a manna that hits the palates of all sorts of people.' Since then they have suffered a spectacular fall from grace. By the time my generation came along they were the mainstay of school dinners, invariably made from a packet and full of ingredients that prescribed ease and convenience, rendering them ugly and tasteless.

Despite such abuses, we still have an enduring affection for these old timers. They have even had a rehabilitation of sorts thanks to the likes of the world's most famous Anglophile: Madonna who claims to have 'a thing about sticky toffee pudding'. An unlikely ambassador for something so heart-stoppingly calorific. I wonder if she ever made one at home.

Most of us never have. During the many conversations I had with friends about such puddings, it became clear that they are seen as too time-consuming to contemplate. Indeed, I was brought up in a household where they never featured, save at Christmas. Until recently, I had never attempted one myself. They are easy. Utterly idiot proof! All you really need is the 2 hours' cooking time. Think about it for a minute – what better way to fill one of those dismal, wintry, Sundays when the last thing you want to do is go anywhere?

I followed Nigella Lawson's advice and bought a plastic pudding basin with a tight-fitting lid. I urge anyone who wants to make a steamed pudding to do the same. No tin foil and cutesy string handles will ever be needed again. The following warning also comes courtesy of Ms Lawson: do not put the lid or the basin in a dishwasher. You will destroy the fit (she thinks of everything).

Golden syrup pudding. **The ultimate in steamed puddings. It must be served with custard.**

For 4 people you need:

50g/2oz butter, softened, plus extra for greasing

100g/3½oz caster sugar

a pinch of salt

4 tbsp milk

2 large eggs

100g/3½oz self-raising flour

juice of ½ lemon

3 tbsp golden syrup

If you have a food processor throw in the butter, sugar, salt, milk, eggs and flour and blitz the mixture until it is smooth. This will not take that long by hand either. It should now be the consistency of a thick batter, but if it is too thick to pour add a little more milk.

Grease a medium-sized pudding basin (approx 1.4litres/2½pints, with a lid) with a little butter. Add the lemon juice to the golden syrup to loosen it, then pour into the base of the pudding basin. Pour the batter on top. I pour from the outside in, in a sort of clockwise swirl, this keeps the heavier syrup at the bottom of the bowl. Cover the basin with the lid.

Boil a kettle full of water. Place the pudding basin into a large saucepan, also with a lid. Fill the saucepan with the boiling water, to come about two-thirds of the way up the sides of the pudding basin. Place on a medium to low flame, cover the pan and simmer for about 2 hours. Make sure that the water does not boil dry. It is unlikely to, but you should check it at least once every 30 minutes and, if necessary, top up with boiling water.

When the pudding is ready, remove it from the pan and allow it to rest for a couple of minutes. Remove the lid (careful of the steam) and place an upturned dish on top of the pudding. Now simply invert both dish and pudding and let the sponge plop gently onto the dish. If you are worried that it won't, by all means run a palette knife around the edge of the basin first.

This pudding, as with all steamed sponges, is best eaten immediately. Because it is generally so hot I prefer to make the custard well in advance and not reheat it. The sad and greedy truth is that this enables you to tuck in fairly swiftly but without burning your tongue too badly.

Spotted Dick. In times gone by this pudding was known as spotted dog. It was like a roly poly: log-shaped and studded with dried fruits. It is hardly surprising that it got (ahem!) renamed. I like to think that someone 'prim and proper' came up with the idea of putting the ingredients into a pudding bowl in an attempt to stifle the sniggers of those at the table. We will never know.

As it turns out, there may have been a more recent attempt at snigger-stifling. Whilst researching this book I came across a cutting from *The Scotsman* newspaper. A journalist was following up a claim that (allegedly!) one well-known retailer, concerned at the dwindling sales of spotted Dick, was going to rename it 'Richard'. Let's hope this was a well-meaning hack falling for a joke or a stab at some publicity by a canny press officer.

The version below is my own. I have tried many 'Olde Worlde' versions and they can be very heavy. Following the fine tradition of pudding puns we could, therefore, call this 'Lesser Spotted Dick'.

For 4 people you need:

50g/2oz butter, softened, plus extra for greasing
2 tbsp brandy
100g/3½oz currants
100g/3½oz caster sugar
2 large eggs
100g/3½oz self-raising flour
a pinch of salt
1 tsp baking powder
2 tbsp milk

Grease a medium-sized pudding basin (approx 1.4litres/2½pints, with a lid) with a little butter and leave to one side.

Warm the brandy until it is just simmering and throw in the currants. Take off the heat and allow to infuse for at least 30 minutes.

Beat the butter and sugar until pale and fluffy, then whisk in the eggs, one by one. Fold in the flour, salt and baking powder. Loosen slightly with the milk, then beat in the currants and any liquid left in their bowl.

This mix is slightly thicker than the batter for other steamed puddings in this chapter, so it will need to be spooned into the pudding basin. Cover the basin with the lid. Boil a kettle full of water. Place the pudding basin into a large saucepan, also with a lid. Fill the saucepan with the boiling water, to come about two-thirds of the way up the sides of the pudding basin. Place on a medium to low flame cover the pan and simmer for about 2 hours. Make sure that the water does not boil dry. It is unlikely to, but you should check it at least once every 30 minutes and, if necessary, top up with boiling water.

Towards the end of the cooking time it is worth sliding a skewer into the top of the pudding, since it can seem denser than the others. If the skewer comes out dry the spotted Dick is ready to eat. Carefully remove the basin from the pan and remove the lid (mind the steam). Place an upturned dish on top of the basin, invert both dish and basin and let the pudding plop gently onto the dish. Serve with custard.

Toenail pie. **Do not be put off by the horrible name. This is a densely sweet, steamed pudding crowned with raspberry jam and sprinkled with desiccated coconut. The little white curls of the coconut are the toenails. It reminded me of how adept my peers were at giving nasty titles to whatever was dished up at school, whether it tasted good or not.**

Whilst researching this book I came across a vast number of people who hate desiccated coconut (my heart goes out to them). It is far from essential in the following recipe. I'm sure it was first added to jazz up a traditional jam and sponge affair. If you dispense with the coconut you can make this pudding with any jam or marmalade that you like. For a real toenail pie it must, must, must be raspberry jam.

For 4 people you need:

50g/2oz butter, softened, plus extra for greasing

100g/3½oz caster sugar

a pinch of salt

4 tbsp milk

2 large eggs

100g/3½oz self-raising flour

juice of ½ lemon

3 tbsp raspberry jam

desiccated coconut (as much or as little as you like)

Grease a medium-sized pudding basin (approx 1.4litres/2½pints, with a lid) with a little butter and put to one side.

If you have a food processor throw in the butter, sugar, salt, milk, eggs and flour and blitz the mixture until it is smooth. This will not take that long by hand either. It should now be the consistency of a thick batter, but if it is too thick to pour add a little more milk.

Add the lemon juice to the jam to loosen it up. Now plonk the jam mixture into the pudding basin and pour the batter over the top. Follow the cooking instructions for the golden syrup pudding on page 184.

Just before serving the pudding, sprinkle the jam with the desiccated coconut. Serve with custard.

A dollop of cream. Cream is one of life's naturally occurring luxuries. When milk is left to stand, fat globules float to the top to form a layer of cream. Before the modern-day practice of helping this process along by creating centrifuges, cream would have been fairly scarce and therefore expensive. Before the days of pasteurization and refrigeration milk could easily spoil in the process. This might be why people contrived other ways to thicken and enrich milk. Custard is one example, but deliberate curdling to make junkets and syllabubs was once common practice.

Nowadays there is a bewildering array of creams available. Which cream you choose to buy depends on what you plan to do with it. For a simple accompaniment to a pudding or pie the best might be the incredibly thick clotted cream, naturally soured cream (or the French crème fraîche) and the pouring kind (single cream). These creams are usually best left in their natural state.

For cooking or whipping I would always choose double or whipping cream. The fat content of these two types has been tampered with deliberately to make them suitable for heating or whisking (you cannot, for instance, whip a single cream). When you whip cream you are rapidly folding air into the fats so that the cream doubles in size and becomes thicker. Mechanized whisks and food processors can make this a lightning quick process, but I still think that whipping is best done by hand. Although it takes longer and requires a fair amount of elbow grease you are much more in control of how thick the cream will end up. It is possible to whip cream for too long so that what you end up with is a buttery mess. This is very easily done if a recipe tells you to whip cream and then fold it into other ingredients. The cream might look just right once whipped, but stirring it again with something else can tip it over the edge. In the following recipes, where whipping cream is required, you should whisk it with fairly long strokes, and not too rapidly, stopping when it just begins to firm up. From there it can finish itself off by standing or by being carefully folded with a spatula or wooden spoon. Adding a very small amount of honey (a teaspoon) will stop whipped cream from deteriorating or drying out when left in the fridge.

To start with here are a few recipes where cream takes the centre stage, with a few simple flavourings.

Lemon creams.

These can be served as a light dessert with home-made shortbread.

For 4–6 people you need:
- 300ml/½ pint double cream
- 150ml/¼ pint single cream
- zest and juice of 1 lemon
- 25g/1oz caster sugar

Place the creams and lemon zest into a saucepan and bring to scalding point – the cream will look like it is about to boil and will fizz against the side of the pan.

Stir in the sugar and the lemon juice. Pour into individual dishes (ramekins are good) and chill for at least 2 hours before serving.

Syllabub.

Syllabub is an ancient word, referring to some of the earliest puddings eaten in Britain. Originally, milk was curdled with wine and the resulting solids were eaten floating on the whey. Once the practice of whipping cream had been developed the curdling no longer took place and the alcohol actually acted as both flavouring and preservative. Syllabubs could then be made and kept in a cool dairy or pantry without spoiling for a day or two. The earliest trifles were almost certainly made by serving syllabub on top of 'tipsy cakes' (bread or sponge impregnated with alcohol) and to this day you can make a fine trifle by using syllabub instead of cream and custard. The recipe that follows is a simple one that is delicious in its own right. It will keep for a few days in the fridge. Make this in individual glasses or a bowl as if you were doing a trifle.

For 4 people you need:
- 2 tbsp honey
- 4 tbsp sherry or brandy
- 1 glass (approx. 200ml/7fl oz) sweet white wine
- finely grated zest of 1 lemon
- 568ml carton double cream

Dissolve the honey in the sherry or brandy and the wine. Add the lemon zest.

Beat the cream until it is just beginning to set, then fold in the honey mixture. Pour into serving bowl(s) and chill until needed.

Serve this with ginger biscuits, which you could make yourself very easily (see page 72).

Orange possets.

This modern-day posset is a set cream, but possets were originally warm frothy drinks, curdled with ale or molasses, and thickened with bread. The following dessert may take its name from the fact that a layer of lighter, frothier cream does manifest itself at the top as it sets.

For 4 people you need:

568ml carton double cream

250g/9oz caster sugar

juice of 3 oranges and the grated zest of 1 orange

juice of 1 lemon

Combine all the ingredients in a pan and bring them to a simmer for 5 minutes. Allow the mixture to cool slightly, then pour into small glasses or ramekins. Leave to set for at least 2 hours before serving.

Rhubarb or gooseberry fool.

A fool is one of the simplest, but finest, puddings in the world. The principle is simple enough – puréed fruit is gently folded into whipped cream. Rhubarb and gooseberries are not only the best fruits for fool, they are so peculiarly English that they add to the whole summer lawn feel of the thing.

I always add custard to my fools, since that is the way I was taught to make them. I love to make my own custard, but since I realize that this can turn fool into a minor chore, you could do worse than buy some in. Not powdered or tinned custard, I'm afraid: you need a fresh one, available in most supermarkets.

For 4 people you need:

500g/1lb 2oz rhubarb or gooseberries, cleaned, trimmed and cut into slices

2 tbsp caster sugar

juice of 1 lemon

125g/4oz fresh custard

250ml/9fl oz double cream

Cook the fruit with the sugar and lemon juice until it has become pulpy. Allow it to cool completely.

At this point you can blitz it in a food processor or leave it rough. Stir in the custard.

Beat the cream separately until it is just beginning to set, then gently fold it into the fruit. I never fold the ingredients together until they are totally homogenous. I like to leave the whole thing slightly 'marbled'. It is totally up to you how you do this.

Strawberries and cream. The rather wistful association of strawberries with the Wimbledon fortnight is now thoroughly old-fashioned thanks to the wide availability of imported strawberries. We think of them as something very British because we have such an appetite for them (why else would those tennis fans pay such ridiculous sums of money for strawberries and cream?) but the domesticated strawberry was originally an import from Virginia. Before that, all European strawberries were wild, and in this country they were a rarity.

The simple combination of strawberries and single cream, sprinkled with caster sugar, is such a fine thing that it needs no embellishment if the strawberries are good. There is a romantic notion, bound up with the memory of strawberries as an early summertime phenomenon, that the English fruit are always perfect, but sadly it isn't so. A late frost or a wet summer can put paid to that. Strawberries are a lottery. They can be beautiful and tasteless, or sweet, but bruised beyond redemption. Macerating them helps sort the flavour and texture out a bit. I leave them, halved and hulled, sitting in a bowl with a squeeze of lemon juice and a tablespoon of sugar, until they begin to bleed. Then, if they are still lousy, I might apply no more than 5 minutes cooking in the resulting juices. The following recipes work equally well with strawberries in their prime or the macerated version.

Strawberry shortcake.

As well as being a great summer pudding, this is my standard for birthday cake. The sandwich part is more biscuity (and foolproof) than a classic Victoria sponge.

For two 20.5cm/8in sandwich cake tins you need:

125g/4oz butter

125g/4oz caster sugar

2 eggs

125g/4oz self-raising flour

The filling:

450g/1lb strawberries, hulled and quartered

50g/2oz caster sugar

100ml/3½fl oz double cream

icing sugar for dusting

Preheat the oven to 180°C/350°F/gas 4.

To make the shortcake, beat the butter and sugar together until pale and fluffy, then beat in the eggs, one at a time. Fold in the flour and divide the mixture between the two sandwich tins. Bake for 25 minutes, then allow them to cool completely before turning them out.

Meanwhile, macerate the strawberries with the sugar for at least 30 minutes.

Whip the cream until it is just beginning to set, then fold in the strawberries. Spread this mixture (the amount should seem very opulent) over one of the two sponges and top it with the other. Dust the top of the cake liberally with icing sugar just before serving.

Eton mess. **How this pudding came to be is a bit of a mystery. It does come from the famous public school and probably dates back to the thirties. Whether or not the broken meringue was originally a mistake hardly matters now, since it is such an essential part of its charm. Eton mess can be made with bananas, but it is most commonly done with strawberries.**

Meringues are quite easy to make, but they do take time. Since what you are going to do is smash up what you've made and literally fold it up with a 'mess' of strawberries and cream, you can use the shop-bought kind, but I do like my meringues slightly gooey in the middle. I've never found a commercially produced meringue that is like this.

For 4 people you need:

2 egg whites
100g/3½oz caster sugar
the tiniest pinch of baking powder (⅛ tsp)
500g/1lb 2oz strawberries, hulled and quartered
squeeze lemon juice
1 tbsp caster sugar
250ml/9fl oz double cream, whipped

Preheat the oven to 150°C/300°F/gas 2. Line a baking sheet with parchment.

To make the meringue, whisk the egg whites until they form soft peaks, then beat in the caster sugar, 1 tablespoon at a time. Allow a good 30 seconds between each spoonful. Then add the baking powder. The meringue is ready to cook when all the sugar has been folded in and what you have looks (not to put too fine a point on it) like shaving foam.

Spoon or pipe it onto the baking sheet in whatever way you like. I just spoon out spatula-sized blobs.

As soon as you put the meringue into the oven turn the heat right down to 140°C/275°F/gas 1 and leave it in there for 2 hours. Then turn off the oven and leave it in until completely cool. Now this should be meringue without angst. If it seems very gooey inside it really isn't a problem for Eton mess.

Meanwhile, macerate the strawberries in the lemon juice and sugar.

To assemble the pudding, I usually take about a third of the strawberries and blitz them to a sauce in a processor, but this is entirely optional. Fold the remaining strawberries with the whipped cream and as much meringue as you like. If you did blitz some of the fruit, top the pudding with the sauce and serve.

Spiffing!

Two puddings with biscuit bases.

Lemon Cotswold. **This is a type of refrigerator cheesecake. It might just be the easiest dessert to make in the world, since everything comes out of a packet. Being a bona fide food snob I have tried to fiddle with the recipe on occasion, using cream instead of evaporated milk, and real gelatine instead of fruit jelly, but the results just aren't the same! This tastes glorious as it is, children love it and it freezes well. If you use commercial lime jelly it will be a mildly disturbing hue of pale green. Fanny Craddock would be proud.**

For a 20.5cm/8in cake tin you need:

75g/3oz butter, melted, plus extra for greasing

100g/3½oz digestive biscuits, crushed

135g box lemon or lime jelly

200ml/7fl oz evaporated milk (half a normal-sized tin)

300g tub cream cheese (like Philadelphia)

juice of 1 lemon

Grease the cake tin. Mix the butter and biscuit crumbs together to make the cake base and press evenly into the tin.

Dissolve the jelly in 100ml/3½fl oz of hot water and set aside.

Whisk or beat the evaporated milk until it thickens. When ready it resembles very lightly whipped cream. Beat in the cream cheese and the lemon juice, then the dissolved jelly. Pour the whole mixture over the biscuit base and chill for at least 2 hours, by which time it will have set.

To release the cake from the tin, dip a palette knife or fish slice in warm water and run it carefully around the edge of the cake.

Variations. If using lime jelly you can also use chocolate digestives for the base. This is delicious.

The original recipe, surely American, included 125g/4oz caster sugar beaten into the cream cheese before it was added to the milk. I have always found this too much, but those with a very sweet tooth might like to try it.

My grandmother's lemon meringue pie.

My grandmother, and consequently my mother, always made lemon meringue pie with a biscuit base. I think it is unbeatable that way. The lemon part in my recipe is very sharp since the meringue and the biscuits are sweet. If you want to sweeten the filling just increase the sugar. It will not really affect the cooking of the eggs.

For a 20.5cm/8in cake tin you need:

The base:

50g/2oz butter, melted, plus extra for greasing

100g/3½oz digestive biscuits, crushed

The filling:

2 egg yolks

2 level tbsp caster sugar

3 level tbsp cornflour

juice and zest of 2 lemons

50g/2oz butter, softened

The topping:

2 egg whites

100g/3½oz caster sugar

Grease the cake tin and line it with parchment.

Make the base. Mix the butter and biscuit crumbs together and press into the base of the cake tin as evenly as possible. Chill the tin in the fridge for 30 minutes.

Preheat the oven to 150°C/300°F/gas 2.

For the filling, whisk the egg yolks with the sugar and cornflour until they are pale and smooth. Put the lemon juice and zest in a saucepan with 200ml/7fl oz of water and bring to the boil. Pour it over the egg mixture, beating constantly until the mixture has dissolved in the water. Pour the lemon mixture into the pan and return to a gentle heat. Cook until thickened, stirring constantly with a wooden spoon. This doesn't take long. It is ready when the spoon leaves a clearly visible 'wake' as you stir. When this happens fold in the butter and pour the mixture into the cake tin.

To make the topping, beat the egg whites until they just start to set and add the caster sugar, one-third at a time, until the mixture forms stiff peaks. Spread this over the lemon mixture and bake the pie for about 40 minutes. The meringue should be browned slightly on top.

I think lemon meringue pie is best served once completely cooled.

Stale bread desserts. These are great standby puds since you are more than likely to have all the ingredients knocking around at any one time. Not that this should be the only justification for including the recipes in a book about comfort eating. They can be rich, sweet and stodgy like Poor Knights of Windsor, or as strangely elegant as a summer pudding. They are also a slice (no pun intended) of culinary history, as the recipe below will illustrate.

Poor Knights of Windsor.

This pudding is truly ancient. There are written instructions for 'Pain Perdu' (the original French name) dating back to 1420. Henry V is supposed to have eaten it, which suggests that the aristocracy's penchant for sticky puddings is nothing new!

The pain in 'Pain Perdu' (literally: 'Hidden Bread') was almost certainly brioche, which I have used before now. I must admit that I find it a little too rich that way, since brioche already contains a mountain of eggs and butter. Panettone, the Italian Christmas bread, works better. Basically, as long as there is stale, white bread around, Poor Knights can be made in minutes.

For all its Olde Worlde credentials it has something of the 'Elvis Presley deep-fried sandwich' about it, which makes it a great midnight feast (see opposite page). It can be done elegantly though, with cream, fresh fruit or jam. Both versions follow.

One more thing: when served warm, it is spectacular with ice cream.

As a pudding for 4 people you need:

100g/3½oz butter

300ml/½ pint milk

2 tbsp sherry

2 tbsp caster sugar

4 slices stale white bread, crusts removed, cut into triangle slices about 2cm/¾in thick (don't worry too much about the measurement)

2 egg yolks

¼ tsp ground cinnamon

First of all it is a good idea to clarify the butter. This is easy. Simply heat it in a small saucepan over a medium flame. As the butter begins to bubble the milk solids will appear as white flecks. Keep an eye on the pan and let the flecks turn a golden colour (it can take between 3–5 minutes) before straining through a cloth or double thickness of kitchen paper.

In a bowl, whisk together the milk, sherry and half the sugar. Soak each slice of bread in this mix and set aside. Beat the egg yolks into the remaining milk mixture in the bowl.

Gently heat the clarified butter in a frying pan or skillet. Dip the bread slices in the egg and milk mixture, then fry gently, turning them until golden on both sides. Lay them on a plate and sprinkle with the remaining caster sugar, plus the cinnamon.

You can serve immediately or keep warm in a low oven until needed. Really, the pudding is so easy that if you have everything ready to hand (including the clarified butter) you can make them to order.

As a midnight feast.

For the purposes of true midnight feasting you could get away with fresh bread. If it is a little pappy give it 1 minute in a toaster, then leave for 10 minutes before using.

As a midnight feast for two:

300ml/½ pint milk

2 egg yolks

2 tbsp golden syrup

2 tbsp sherry

2 tbsp butter

2 slices stale white bread (or toast, see above), crusts removed, each cut into 4 triangles

1 tbsp caster sugar

¼ tsp ground cinnamon (optional)

In a small saucepan (a milk pan is ideal), whisk together the milk, eggs, golden syrup and sherry. Dip the bread in this mixture slice by slice and put to one side.

Gently heat the butter in a frying pan or skillet. For this version you may wish to skip clarifying and, to tell the truth, there is something a little sexy about the caramelized bits of butter you get on the bread.

Fry the slices of bread until browned and a little crispy. Put them on a plate and sprinkle with the sugar and cinnamon (if using).

Now, it is more than likely that, sitting in the milk pan, is the remaining egg/milk mixture, just waiting to be turned into midnight-feast type custard. Whisk in hand, start to gently beat the mixture over a medium heat. Because of the sherry it will go a little frothy, which is lovely. As soon as there is any thickening to the mix (and it takes about a minute – you will feel it through the whisk) remove from the heat and quickly tip it into a bowl. This is great for dipping the Poor Knights in. It also makes you look quite a dab hand in the kitchen, especially at this hour.

Bread and butter pudding.

There is no finer use for a slice of stale bread. I have seen recipes using Panettone or chocolate croissants. I have even made it with hot cross buns. The basic principle of cooking any of the above with the eggs and cream is open to all sorts of permutations because it is very flexible. My friend John makes the best. This is his recipe.

For 4 people you need:

8 slices of stale white bread spread with soft butter

50g/2oz mixed dried fruit

3 eggs

2 level tbsp caster sugar

2 drops vanilla essence

200ml/7fl oz whole milk

100ml/3½fl oz double cream

2 tbsp soft brown sugar (optional)

Preheat the oven to 180°C/350°C/gas 4.

Cut the bread into soldiers. Arrange the bread and fruits in a small baking dish or ovenproof bowl until you have a sort of lattice.

Beat the eggs with the sugar and vanilla, then beat in the milk and cream. Pour this over the bread and sprinkle the top with the brown sugar (if using). Now press the pudding slightly so that the top of it gets 'sogged' as well as the bottom. Leave the pudding to rest in a cool place for at least 1 hour. Bake for about 30 minutes, then allow to rest for 10 minutes before serving as the pudding will continue to set without the eggs overcooking.

Summer pudding. **This is a very elegant pudding that needs to be made a good day before eating to really shine. I'm afraid that I think it is best made with the most plastic sliced white bread you can get your mitts on, since the slicing has been so perfectly, homogeneously done by machine! Now at the risk of trashing all association between this pudding and countryside quaintness, I also have to tell you that I have found that the readily available bags of frozen summer fruits you can buy in most supermarkets are unbeatable for a summer pudding. There is no destalking or hulling to do and as the fruits thaw they macerate themselves, giving you plenty of juices to make the pudding with. They are also very economical, since you need quite a lot of fruit.**

For an averaged-sized (1.5 litre/2½ pint) pudding bowl you need:

800g/1lb 12oz mixed summer fruits

200g/7oz caster sugar

1 bag stale sliced white bread, crusts removed

If using raw fruit, cook it with the caster sugar for about 10 minutes and set aside until completely cooled. Strain them and reserve all the juices. If using the frozen berries, thaw them with the sugar over a strainer, with a bowl to catch all the juices beneath.

Line the inside of the pudding bowl with clingfilm and then the bread. You will want to cut a circular piece to line the base of the bowl. Then you can press the slices into the sides until they are completely covered. Don't leave any gaps. Pour all the fruit into the bowl and add about two-thirds of the juices. Keep some aside to pour over the top later. Now cover the base of the bowl with more clingfilm and stand a weight like a tin on the base. Chill overnight.

To serve the pudding, remove the clingfilm from the base and invert the bowl over a wide plate. Tap the bowl a few times and the pudding should plop very gently away from the bowl – you will hear it happen. Keep tapping if not, or walk away and let gravity do the trick. If any of the bread hasn't caught the juices and gone a dark shade of 'berry', spoon over the remaining juices. Serve with single cream.

Here is my friend Carla's wonderful posh (her words!) and slightly Italianate summer pudding:

Substitute half the fruit for 250g/9oz mascarpone and line the pudding bowl with stale Madeira cake instead of bread. Wet the cake once it is pressed into the bowl with some of the berry juices and reserve the rest to spoon over the top when turned out. Combine the fruit with the mascarpone and caster sugar and use that as the filling. Something else!

Baked plums and port. **This is a lovely pudding with a dollop of clotted cream. It is perfect if you can't face the thought of anything heavy or super sweet at the end of a meal. For sheer effect you can alternate red and yellow plums in the same tray. If you are cooking a roast, have the plums ready to pop in the oven as you remove the meat and simply adjust the oven temperature.**

For 4 people you need:

8 plums (i.e. 2 per person), halved and stoned

200ml/7fl oz port, or red wine and a splash of cooking brandy

100ml/3½fl oz blood orange juice

2 tbsp caster sugar

Preheat the oven to 180°C/350°F/gas 4.

Put the plums in a baking tray, insides up. Pour over the port (or red wine and brandy) and orange juice, then sprinkle the entire contents of the tray with the caster sugar. Bake the plums, uncovered for about 30 minutes.

Rhubarb crumble. **Crumbles are possibly the best pudding you could ever attempt if the thought of pastry-cooking stresses you out. Crumble topping is like a pie crust without any need for a rolling pin or the like. Besides there being no other winter warmer like a crumble, it is a great pudding to follow a Sunday roast (if you have any room for it!) since it can be made up in advance and popped in the oven while you enjoy the main course.**

Everyone has their favourite crumble, but mine is rhubarb. I think of it as a winter fruit ever since I developed an addiction to the forced Yorkshire rhubarb of the cold months, grown in the dark, in sheds. The result is a surreally pink fruit that you sometimes hear referred to as the champagne of rhubarb. Hunt it out this winter.

For 4–6 people you need:

The fruit:

600g/1lb 5oz rhubarb, cut into chunks

juice and zest of 1 orange

50g/2oz caster sugar

My favourite crumble topping:

100g/3½oz cold butter

200g/7oz plain flour

25g/1oz (about a handful) porridge oats

100g/3½oz golden caster sugar

Preheat the oven to 180°C/350°F/gas 4.

Put the rhubarb, orange juice and zest and sugar in a saucepan and simmer very gently for no more than about 10 minutes. It should still be firm. If lots of juice has formed drain away a good half of it so that what you have is slightly stewy and not soupy.

Meanwhile, make the topping. Rub the butter with the flour and oats until you have a very gravelly-looking mixture. Fold in the sugar.

Now simply place the fruit in a pie or baking dish, top it with the crumble and bake for 30–40 minutes, or until the topping is golden brown.

Alternative fillings:

For gooseberries: Use 800g/1lb 12oz gooseberries, hulled but left whole, the same quantity of sugar and the juice of 1 lemon. Cook the gooseberries for no more than 10 minutes in a small pan before transferring them to the baking dish. Bake as above.

For apple and blackberry: Use 2 good-sized cooking apples, peeled, cored and sliced, plus about 450g/1lb blackberries, washed and left whole. Add 50g/2oz caster sugar and the juice of 1 lemon. Toss the ingredients together, but do not precook them. Bake as above.

For plums: Use 800g/1lb 12oz plums, stoned and quartered, plus 50g/2oz caster sugar, a drop of vanilla essence or ½ vanilla pod and a splosh of red wine. This is delicious. Again, cook the fruit for about 10 minutes before transferring to the baking dish. Bake as above.

You can't leave me alone. **Scouring recipe books, archives and the many emails I received whilst writing *Just like mother used to make* unearthed some great oddities. At the end of the day, these are what comfort food is all about for most of us. I want to end this section, and in fact this book, with a 'mystery pudding' hiding at the back of my grandmother's handwritten cookbook. She kept this book, amending and updating it constantly, through the busy years of her married life. My grandfather ran a Methodist chapel and hostel in London's Walworth and 'Annan' (as she was known by everyone) was a keen cook, producing endless lunches, dinners and teas for a steady stream of visitors. No-one in my family can recall where this pudding originated or how it got its name. If the proof of all puddings is, as they say, in the eating, the reasons for the title are obvious.**

Here then, is the enigmatic 'you can't leave me alone', dedicated to my wonderful Annan, who I wish could have seen this book. I think she would have both recognized and enjoyed nearly all of it. Either that or had me done for flagrant plagiarism. This is best served in glasses, but you can serve it in a bowl.

For 4 people you need:
3 eggs, separated
50g/2oz caster sugar
zest and juice of 1 lemon
1 drop vanilla essence
5 leaves of gelatine
50g/2oz raspberry jam
100ml/3½fl oz double cream, whipped

Beat the egg yolks and sugar until pale and fluffy, then add the lemon zest and vanilla essence.

Beat the egg whites until they form stiff peaks.

Dissolve the gelatine in 1 tablespoon of warm water and add it to the egg yolks, then fold in the whites.

Loosen the jam with the lemon juice and drop a small amount into each glass or a small bowl.

Fill each glass or bowl two-thirds of the way up with the egg mixture and allow to set in the fridge for about 2 hours. Once set top the pudding with the whipped cream and serve immediately.